COCKTAILS
WITH GOD

For more information about
COCKTAILS WITH GOD
www.CocktailsWithGod.com

COCKTAILS

WITH GOD

Featuring 22 Heavenly Drink Recipes

A NOVEL BY
DAVID TRIEMERT

ONE LIGHT PRESS

Cocktails With God™

ISBN 0-9727446-1-4

Printed in the United States of America.

One Light Press
P.O. Box 97
Afton, MN 55001
(651) 436-5959

www.onelightpress.com

To My Pride and Joy!

Danielle

To contact the author:
davidtriemert@hotmail.com

Acknowledgments

In writing this book I drew from a lifetime of experiences, both good and not so good, but all of value and necessary for my journey through life. With that I thank equally my family and friends, critics and foes.

In what I consider to be Divine Providence, many teachers were sent my way over the years, both in person and in print—you know who you are, and I thank you for it.

To Nickie Dillon, my editor, and Benjamin DeLeon, my graphic artist—thank you, thank you!

To everyone else who helped shape and form this book, both directly and indirectly, including those who reviewed the first draft, or wrote the cocktail recipes, and shared in all the fun of test-driving the drinks: Deborah Lynn Murphy, Kate Foley, Sue Gifford DeLeon, Gary Atkinson, Don and Sue Bauer, Donna Tveten, KaCey Syring, Lisa Powers, Marcia Jedd, Julie Hall, Phyllis (Space) Kaplan, Lida Gifford, Heather Heinn, Thersa Tauer, Käri Niessink, Jaqueline Books, Dan Koppes, Becky Heinn, Brian DeLeon, Doug Harvey, Sharon McPheron, Dierdre Beck, Jim DeNoble, James Migues, Elizabeth Castellanos, Lee Bucci, Jerry, John and Rona Gigliotti, Lee Angers, Joe and Sue Molnar, John Shelton, Roxanne Morin, Charlotte Spicer. Cheers!

Finally, to the late comedian Sam Kinison, whose "message" influenced many lives, including my own.

Contents

Heavenly Drink Recipes

Appetizers

*"Everyone wants to go to heaven,
but no one wants to die."*

Anonymous

Dear Reader

If God invites you over for cocktails, but the only way to join him is to die...will you?

I did, and I have to say that waking up in Heaven each morning to accompany God on these long drinking bouts that last till late at night is more fun than I ever could have imagined. And in the days ahead, you will join me, whether you drink or not. I saw your name on the guest list—your invitation is being prepared.

"But what should I wear to the party?" you may ask.
Don't worry about it. Come as you are.

"And will I know anyone there?" you question.
Yes, dead celebrities by the score, and all of your relatives who have previously crossed over, including those who owe you money and those you owe money to.

"Need I bring anything, like a gift or a bottle?"
Just your Soul. Everything else is provided.

"How long does it last?"
I can't say, but plan on spending the night.

"Will it be any fun?"
People lay down their lives to attend.

I can't wait to see you. Gotta go.

Sincerely,
Buddy Wilde

P.S. Don't forget to RSVP.

"Be not forgetful to entertain strangers, for some have entertained angels, unaware."

Hebrews 13:2

CHAPTER 1

Going Home

Getting up each day and having cocktails with God is more fun than I ever could have dreamed, but having to actually die in order to join him on these long drinking bouts was a complete nightmare. Upon hearing the news that I had, in fact, exited my lifeless body and checked into Heaven, I wanted nothing more than to turn in my key and wake up in my own bed.

"Good morning, Mr. Wilde," I heard a voice say. "How are you feeling?"

"My head is killing me—like it's in a vice—and I can't see. What happened?" I asked, totally afraid.

"We'll get to that later," the voice said. "Do you know where you are?"

"I think so, but who are you?"

"My name is Tucker. I'm your spirit guide. Welcome to Heaven, Buddy."

"What!" I sat straight up in bed. "What in the hell are you talking about? Get me a goddamned doctor—I need to be looked at." I thought for sure that a mental patient was on the loose and was now playing psychiatrist with me.

"Settle down, Buddy, you're not on Earth anymore," he said. "You suffered a ruptured aneurysm in your brain and crossed over to the other side."

"Other side of what, the hospital? Someone must have screwed up my paperwork and sent me off to the nut ward! Who's in charge around here? I want to talk to someone about this!"

"Sorry, Buddy, but I'm all you've got right now. Can you answer some questions for me?"

Not certain of what actually happened, or where I was other than I knew it wasn't home in my own bed, I decided to play along with this guy claiming to be my spirit guide, as he seemed to be my only access to information for the time being.

"What do you want to know?" I asked him.

"I need to ask some questions, Buddy. Please tell me everything you can remember about the past twenty-four hours." His inquiry was followed by a loud gasp for air and then a gurgling noise.

"Jesus Christ! Go blow your nose or cough up a lung first. How gross."

"Wasn't me. That's a guy in the next bed over."

"Well, then, either open his airway or stick a cork in it. I'm not going to listen to that all night. Find him another room," I snapped.

"Buddy, it's only temporary. Now again, please tell me everything you can remember about the past twenty-four hours."

I thought back for a moment, trying to block out the ungodly sounds coming from the guy next to me, then laid back down before answering his question.

I began, "Okay, I got up this morning and went to work. I'm tearing down an old court house in the historical district to make room for a new library, and it turned out to be a day from hell."

"Can you elaborate?" Tucker asked of me.

"If you insist."

"I do, thank you," he responded.

"All right, let's see…I operate a big crane and was having a hard time knocking down an exterior wall. I'd been pounding on it for a while, but it wouldn't drop. So, I throttled up and swung that baby around doing a full 360-degree turn with the boom, and just before the wrecking ball hit its intended target, the wall somehow collapsed on its own and the momentum from the swing carried the steel ball right through the roof of the church next door."

"O my Lord!" Tucker sighed.

"That's what I said, but you should have seen when the priest and a nun came running out with nothing on, playing tug-of-war over a bed sheet. It looked as if the wrath of God was upon them."

"Our Father works in mysterious ways. What happened after that?" he asked.

"Let's see…I went to the bar, met up with some of the guys from work and drank until closing."

"You did? And drove home after that, under the influence?" he asked.

"No, I skipped all the way home...it's only fifteen miles—of course I drove home!"

"Buddy, you should have had someone give you a ride," he said.

Not being in any mood to be lectured about drinking and driving, I shot back, "I made it home safe, right? And staying out all night at the bar with my friends is certainly not why I am here."

"But you could have hurt or killed someone!"

"Listen," I said to Tucker, "I know when I can drive and when I can't. I'm not like some people who get all boozed up and then try to drive home with one eye closed. I take drinking and driving very seriously, and if I have any question whatsoever about my ability to responsibly operate a vehicle, I don't drive...period, end of discussion!"

Tucker wasn't finished. "But you shouldn't even be on the road if you've been drinking alcohol."

"Hey, I don't know where you come from, but in the town where I live, half the people on the road shouldn't be allowed to drive, even when they're sober! When I get behind the wheel after a night out on the town, the music dies and the party stops before I even open my car door. And in the event it doesn't, I either find a ride or hide my keys in the grass and take a nap."

"But what about last night?" he asked.

"Six beers over the course of eight hours? Figure it out!" I yelled.

Just then a demanding voice came over the loudspeaker in the room and asked, "Who goes there?"

Tucker responded to the voice, "It's just me."

The voice on the loudspeaker shouted, "Keep it down, dammit—it's after-hours."

"Who in the world was that?" I asked.

Tucker hesitated and then replied, "The last one you ever want to get on the bad side of, Buddy."

"He sounds like a real ass to me, and I'm sure glad I don't work here, because I'd end up telling him where to get off," I shouted.

"I heard that," the voice on the loudspeaker said.

"So what? It's true!" I shouted back. "Who in the world does that guy think he is anyway—'God,' for Christ's sake?"

Tucker, doing everything he could trying not to laugh at his disbelief with my expression, said, "That's exactly who you were talking to, Buddy, the Almighty himself."

"O boy, not good," I thought to myself, figuring that either Tucker wasn't telling me the truth and could no longer be trusted, or I had just landed myself on the wrong side of an angry God who was already mad at the world, and now me in particular.

Nervous with the thought of being in either predicament, I reasoned that I was still in my life on Earth and was just having a bad dream, so I said to Tucker, "Cut all the bullshit and finish up with your patchwork here. I'm tired and want to go home, now!"

"I'd like to do that for you, Buddy," he said, "but I can't. And besides, I have more questions to ask."

"Then ask God. He's supposed to be the one with all the answers." And with that, I closed my eyes and nodded off, somehow confident that everything would be back to normal when I woke up again.

Nazarene

Location, Vocation, Damnation.

Fill a tall shaker glass with ice. Add a few drops of dry vermouth and a teaspoon of juice from the olive jar. Next, add 2 shots of gin for the "Crucified" version, or 2 shots of vodka for the "Resurrected" version. Stir and strain into a chilled martini glass. Garnish with a cocktail onion and a garlic-stuffed olive.

*"There is nothing either good or bad
but thinking makes it so."*

William Shakespeare, *Hamlet*, Act II, Scene 2

Angel Wings

Chicken wings that died of curry.

2 lbs. chicken wings
½ lb. butter
14 oz. bottle Louisiana Hot Sauce
1 tablespoon curry powder
1 cup finely ground cashews

1. Place butter in a bowl and allow to soften.
   Add Louisiana Hot Sauce and mix well.
2. In a separate bowl, combine finely ground
   cashews with curry powder. Mix well.
3. Deep-fry chicken wings in oil until golden
   brown. Next, place the wings in the bowl with
   butter/hot sauce, while still warm, folding
   into mixture and stirring until well coated.
4. Remove wings from sauce one-by-one and
   roll in mixture of cashews and curry powder.

CHAPTER 2

One Nasty Hangover

"Buddy, Buddy, you have to wake up," Tucker said to me, shaking my arm. "I need to ask you some more questions."

"What's this?" I thought. "Maybe it's not a dream."

"I have to know," he said, "when you got home from the bar, did you sleep through the night?"

"No," I said, making him well aware of my displeasure at his having woken me up.

He persisted. "Buddy, I need you to work with me. Please answer my questions with as much detail as you can. I'm trying to help you through this."

"Okay, I'll tell you, but then leave me the hell alone." I told him how I got up around three in the morning with a splitting headache, put on my pants, went out to the kitchen for some aspirin and a drink of water, then blacked out. That's all I remembered.

"Please continue," he said, "it's important. What happened after that?"

I thought back for a few seconds and then said, "From there, I guess I woke up here sometime later, but I wasn't really awake. It's like I was in a dream state, floating around up at the ceiling and I could see what looked like my body on a long, skinny table with a half-dozen people around me. It was chaotic. One guy was pounding on my chest, another tried desperately to jam a plastic tube down my throat, someone else was sticking a needle in my arm, while a fourth person shaved my head."

"And after that?" Tucker asked.

"Well, the next thing I remember was hearing a woman shout, 'We're losing him. He's not going to make it if we don't get in there now!' Then there was the sound of a power tool, followed by a terrible vibration on my scull, and a short time later the guy who'd been trying to get my heart going said, 'Dammit, he's gone. Elvis has left the building.' What'd he mean by that, anyway?"

"It doesn't matter. Go on," Tucker said, prompting me to finish my story, knowing full well that the doctor had implied that my spirit had left my body.

"And then, the coolest thing happened...a brilliant white light appeared. I'd seen this light before—when I was almost killed in a motorcycle accident—but this time it was even brighter and I was drawn to it just like the first time. Finally, I woke up here to the sound of your voice.

Please tell me I'm all right and that you expect me to make a full recovery." My spirit guide didn't respond right away to the question.

"I love my job," Tucker began, "except for when I must deliver unpleasant news."

"What are you trying to say?" I asked him, feeling great concern.

"That splitting headache you complained of waking up to, Buddy?"

"Yeah…" I responded slowly, wanting to delay his next words, which could contain the bad news that no one cares to hear.

"It was the effect of a ruptured artery in your brain. They hurt."

"And…?" I said, proceeding cautiously.

"Well, Buddy, the odds of surviving a condition this severe are not favorable."

"I'm not liking this." I sat up.

"I can tell. However, they brought you into the ER, rushed you into surgery and—to make a long story short—the doctors did everything in their power to bring you back, but it didn't work out."

"What…didn't work out?" I asked, now expecting to hear the worst.

"The operation, Buddy. It was a very complicated procedure and with the extended period of time that passed before you even reached the hospital, it would have taken an Act of God to save your life, but…"

"But what?" I demanded, somehow expecting to be let down.

"He was busy at the time."

"Who's 'He'?" I asked.

"God," Tucker replied.

"God? God was 'busy'? I don't believe it!"

"What can I say, Buddy? That was his response," Tucker said.

"Busy doing what?" I asked, my fear quickly turning to anger. "Beating up an old lady for missing a day in church?"

"Be careful," Tucker warned me.

"Well, come on, the God I know doesn't have limitations. Are we talking about the same God?"

"There's only one."

"Then why am I dead? You are telling me that I am dead, right?"

"No, you're not dead," Tucker replied. "You merely crossed over is all. Spirit never dies, Buddy, it only moves from one dimension to the next and then back again."

"I don't believe this shit! Dead at the ripe old age of thirty-five—unbelievable! Is that what you are telling me?" My spirit guide went silent, giving me a moment to stop and think, try to make sense of it all.

After reflecting back on this whole turn of events for what seemed like an eternity, and coming to the conclusion that I could in fact be dead, I asked, "So, what happens now, Tucker, I mean, with my daughter? How is she going to deal with all this?"

"Don't worry about her," he said. "She'll be all right, as will your family and friends. You'll see them again, I promise."

"But how will they get along without me?" I asked, wanting to break down and cry.

"Oh, they'll survive, Buddy. That's why they're called 'survivors.' Of course, there's a process of mourning they will have to go through, due to their loss with your being gone, but they will be just fine, for the most part."

"For the most part?" I blurted out. That didn't sound all-inclusive. "Will some people get over my passing better than others?"

"Humans are a funny bunch," Tucker said, with a tone of laughter and disbelief. "Most take the death of a loved one and themselves to be final when, in reality, it's just part of a continuum."

"A what?"

"A continuum."

"Never heard of it. Sounds like some rare disease."

"The continuum of eternity, Buddy. It's a process where the stages of birth, life and death keep repeating over and over again—we're all subject to it."

Still confused with this whole business of a continuum, as he called it, I thought back on my life and became mindful of the fact that somehow I knew that there was an afterlife, but when I tried to explain this to my spirit guide, he cut me off before I could finish.

"Not hardly," Tucker said. "For a number of years, you didn't believe in the spirit world, life after death, or reincarnation. You only hoped that these things existed. Instead, you were taught at an early age that when a person dies, their soul travels to a holding area where it waits to be judged by a supreme being who seals the soul's fate, directing it to an eternal life in Heaven or Hell. But that's not how it works."

"Are you certain?" I asked.

"Without a doubt, Buddy," he replied.

Leaning back against the pillow beneath my head, thinking about how my life on Earth had been cut short, my mind drifted off to thoughts of my daughter and how my relationship with her mother (who was now my ex) had recently started to improve when the two of us finally agreed that it would be in our little girl's best interest if we could put our failed relationship and differences aside and start acting like parents again, so that this precious little soul we both loved with all of our hearts could have a fighting chance at growing up to live a normal life.

Then I felt an emptiness begin to grow inside me for the love my daughter and I had started to share again, and all the fun we were having on the weekends. I cried out, "How will she ever get along without me, Tucker? Who's going to support and protect her, educate her on the ways of the world, and pick her up when she falls down?"

"I can't honestly answer that, Buddy," he said.

I continued, "And who's going to pay her college tuition when she gets older?"

"I don't know what to tell you, Buddy, but I'm sure she'll figure something out."

"Yeah, that's easy for you to say. But you probably don't have kids. The world keeps getting tougher and tougher each day."

"It wouldn't hurt to ask God about it and have him look after her well-being."

"As if that's going to help. You can see where all of my prayers got me—dead! I didn't even live long enough to experience a midlife crisis, Tucker."

"Your whole life was a crisis," he reminded me.

I settled down a bit and said, "That's true, and it seemed as if the Angel of Death was always right on my tail, but I had no idea that I would run out of breath this early in the game." I laid back down again and tried not to think about what the future might look like in the years ahead for my daughter.

Tucker left my bedside and went over to check on the guy next to me, who much to my surprise was still doing the death rattle, but I had totally forgotten about him, as I had been preoccupied with my own set of circumstances. Then, focusing my attention on the rhythm of his gasp-and-gurgle breathing, I had to ask, "Why's he here, Tucker?"

"Same reason you are, Buddy," he said.

"What I meant was how did he die? He is dead, isn't he?"

"No," Tucker responded, "he just crossed over is all, like you did, but I really shouldn't talk about it. Information of that nature is strictly confidential."

"Then tell me this...providing you're at liberty to talk about it." I thought it to be rather petty of Tucker to be so tightlipped with how a dead guy died, so I asked him in a sarcastic tone, "What's next, Tucker? You know, where do I go from here?"

Tucker paused for a moment and then said, "I hate to have to tell you this, Buddy..."

"What now?" I questioned him, somehow suspecting that the other shoe hadn't dropped yet.

I heard Tucker tell the guy next to me to get some rest, then he came over to me and said, "You're not going to like this, Buddy. However, it is required that you now complete your Life Review, and I must warn you in advance that it's a process that brings forth a great deal of pain, both mentally and emotionally. I'm sorry, Buddy."

I was tempted to whack myself upside the head a few times, just to make sure I was hearing him right. "Pain?" I repeated to myself, more than once.

"For your information, Tucker, just in case you didn't notice, my head is killing me, I can't see, I'm being jerked around by a strange voice who claims to be my 'spirit guide,' and I just died a short time ago, leaving behind a daughter I love more than life itself. Isn't that enough 'pain' for one day?" I gave it my all to try and reason with him.

He responded, "That's how God designed it, Buddy.

He wants you to experience, in a similar fashion, every bit of pain that you have caused others over the course of your lifetime."

I still couldn't believe what I was hearing. "Are you guys insane, or what?!" I shouted. "I just died. I'm dead, spelled D-E-A-D. It's over, my life is over, and you want to toy with me? This isn't Heaven—this is Hell," I said with complete conviction.

"Not true," he argued, "Earth is the only physical hell in the universe, but it can also be a state of mind right here on the other side. It's your choice." It sounded as if my spirit guide was beginning to lose his compassion toward me.

"My choice, my ass, Tucker. I went straight to Hell, didn't I? And you want me to believe that I'm off to see the wizard when, in fact, I'm walking down the corridor to Satan's theme park. Well, here's to you, asshole—fuck you, fuck God, and fuck all the holy bastards, Jesus Christ excluded! I ain't taking no shit from anyone! I'm just going to lie here and hope to hell that I fall asleep and never wake up again."

Tucker countered, "But you haven't completed Life Review, which you must do before you can meet the Almighty. It can't be done any other way!"

"Hey, Tucker, here's some breaking news. I don't want to meet God and listen to his bullshit, either, not if he's the same prick-from-hell that came over the loudspeaker when I first woke up. I'd just as soon rot in Hell for all of eternity!"

Tucker, being completely dumbfounded, told me to lie down and go to sleep.

"There is no death, only a change of worlds."

Chief Seattle
Quoted in *The Spiritual Legacy of the
American Indian* – Joseph Epes Brown

Wing and a Prayer

It's what you need when all else fails.

In a blender, place ½ cup of fresh strawberries, 1½ shots of vodka, 1 shot of Amaretto liqueur and 2 teaspoons of grenadine. Mix well. Then add 1 cup of shaved ice and blend until slushy. Serve in a large margarita glass.

Afterlife

You'll want to have one of these.

Fill an old-fashioned glass with ice. Mix 2 shots of Bailey's Irish Cream with 1 shot of peppermint schnapps. Top with a light splash of club soda.

CHAPTER 3

A Conversation With God

I thought I was home in bed when I woke to the sound of a phone ringing. Tucker could be heard whispering to the guy next to me.

"Get the phone!" I yelled. A moment later he picked it up.

"Receiving. Tucker speaking."

"Oh, hi, glad you could call (pause). Yes, he's here. You want to speak with Buddy Wilde... just a moment, I'll put him on." Tucker nudged me on the arm to signal that the phone was for me.

"Take a message and hold all my calls. I don't want to talk with anyone right now," I said.

"But it's God and he wants to have a word with you, Buddy."

"Tell him I'm in a meeting right now, discussing ways to head off the next natural disaster."

"It's the Father. He wants to talk to you, Buddy."

"I don't believe this shit...*Hello!*"

"Hi, Buddy, it's God. Just called to say 'Welcome

home!'" In the background I could hear a large crowd going nuts. The caller must have taken a recorded sound bite from a rock concert and replayed it with perfect timing.

"I'm sorry, but I don't know anyone named God. You must have me confused with someone else." I had to hold the phone away from my ear because the laughter was almost deafening.

"Really, honestly, I swear to God (the caller was cracking up), it's me, God. You know, the Alpha, the Omega, the…"

"Yeah, yeah, and this is your son, but you reached me at a bad time. I've got five thousand people at the front door complaining of hunger pains. I have to go fishing." The laughter turned hysterical.

"No, no, wait a minute, Buddy. It's me, really."

"Sure it is…prove it!" I challenged.

"All right, I will. Hang on, I want to get you off the speakerphone…ah, that's better. Let's see now…if I can remember how to do this again (the caller was trying to control his laugh). It's been a while…give me a second. Okay, Buddy…the incision on your head, it's still there, correct?"

"Are you referring to the chainsaw wound from the operation?"

"Yes, that's it. I'm going to make it disappear."

"I'd much rather you made me go away, as in 'back to my life on Earth.'"

"No, not yet, Buddy. One thing at a time. Are you ready?" God spoke a few words in a language I'd never heard before and then asked me, "How's your head now?"

"Well, it still hurts…but, hey…the gash is gone. How'd you do that?"

"Ancient Chinese secret," he said with a laugh.

"But it still hurts," I complained, telling him that if he really was who he said he was, I wouldn't be feeling any pain whatsoever.

"It does? Let me try something else." It sounded as if he pounded the phone against a hard surface a few times and then asked, "Is that any better?"

"Who'd ever believe it!" I exclaimed. "There's no pain whatsoever, and it's not numb, either. You're pretty good. What did you say your name was?"

"It's God, dammit," he said, cracking up.

I had to stop and think. This could very well be God, but something isn't right here, I thought to myself, so I asked him, "Have you been drinking?"

"Of course, Buddy," he said proudly. "What else would you expect me to be doing?"

"I don't know. Looking after the world, perhaps?"

"Actually, there's going to be a big party tonight," he said. "A bunch of the guys stopped by to help get things set up. You need to be there."

"Really?" I said. Then I explained to him that if he would be so kind as to fix my eyes so I could see again, I'd probably drop in for a few minutes.

"Oh, that's right," he said. "I totally forgot about...just a second." God pulled the phone from his ear and yelled out as if talking to the crowd, "Anyone seen Boy Wonder? Hey, Peter, where's Jesus? He left? Where did he go? I need an eye specialist, stat! (Pause) What's he doing at the liquor store? We're out of tonic? All right, never mind then." God came back on the line.

"I wanted my son to handle this. He's the healer in the family. That kid can fix anything!"

"That's what I've heard, God. But why is he out

buying something he could probably make on his own? I thought he was the big wine maker."

"Not so much any more, ever since I had to bail him and the Dirty Dozen out of detox one night."

"No way! What happened?"

"Ah…they were whooping it up and he started showing off to some chicks that were over. Created a new cocktail called the Near Death Experience. It ended up kicking their asses, but good."

"What was in it?" I asked, very curious to know.

"I'm not sure, but I want to say embalming fluid was the main ingredient, if that tells you anything."

"Sounds killer!"

"It is!" he said. "Causes immediate death, makes the heart flat-line, which sends them out-of-body, where they re-experience the tunnel, the white light, the peace and love of yours truly…it was a cheap knockoff of the real thing."

"Unbelievable!" I exclaimed.

"Yeah. When they came in, Receiving was in total chaos. No one over there knew what to do, so they ended up getting thrown in the puker."

"Wow," I said, "what if someone on Earth came up with the same idea and bottled it?"

"They'd be ringing my doorbell," he said.

"So what then? You went and took away his ability to perform miracles?" I asked.

"No, Buddy. I just told him to stay out from behind the damned bar is all, but that went over like the Ten Commandments."

"Interesting."

"Say, before you hang up, God—my eyes, can you help me see again? I'd like to crash that party."

"Let me call you back," he said. "I was hoping Jesus would have returned by now, and I need another drink. I'll call you right...oh, wait, someone here wants to talk with you. Hold on."

"Hello?"

I heard a loud scream. "Ah...ahhhhhhhhhhhhhh, how the hell are you, Wild One?"

"Who's this? I think you broke my eardrum!"

"It's Sam Kinison...ah...ahhhhhhhhhhhhhhhh!" he screamed again.

"You've got to be kidding me! That yell, I'd recognize that yell any—is it really you, Sam?"

"It's really me, brother. How are you doing, Buddy?"

"I'm all right, and you?" I was a big admirer of his work as a comedian, but I had never actually met or talked with him before.

He replied, "Oh, man, couldn't be better. I'm in Heaven, thank God."

"I don't believe it! Where?" I asked, hoping I'd get to finally meet him in person.

"I'm over at God's house. There's gonna be a big bash tonight. Welcome home, Buddy!"

"I can't believe it. I mean, I thought for sure you would have gone straight to Hell, Sam—no passing Go, no collecting $200, none of that shit!"

"Oh, them...you can't believe a word those controlling, over-religious bastards say. Hell is where you just came from, Buddy. When we die and leave Earth," he said, "there's only one flight path leading out of the physical plane and it's nonstop—drops you off at God's doorstep."

"That's weird, Sam. I must have taken a connecting flight, because I seem to be on a layover in Receiving. Any idea where I am from you?"

"You're just a few minutes away, my friend, two at the most, but you're inside the pearly gates and that's all that matters. Ah…ahhhhhhhhhhhhhhhhhhhhhhhh! Nice to have you back, Wilde."

"And it's good to hear your voice, Sam. We all miss you, even your critics. They haven't had anything worth a blind date to talk about since your death, Sam. What happened out there, anyway?"

"O man…not now. Maybe we can talk about it at the party. God's waiting to get back on the line with you. Later, dude. Ah…Ahhhhhhhhhhhhhhhhhhhhhhhh!"

God came back on the phone.

"O that damned yell of his, scares the holy Christ out of everyone around here. Thank God I made only one Sam. He's excited to have you home again."

"I see that."

"He's watched you religiously through the Earthcam now for over five years, Buddy. Never missed an opportunity to see you in action. You were as entertaining for him as he was for you."

"The 'Earthcam'?" I asked.

"Twenty-five cents for three minutes, Buddy. It's a technology I developed. Allows you to zoom in on planet Earth and view anything your heart desires, and I mean anything," he said, as if smiling.

"That's scary," I said, not liking the sound of that.

Then God spoke. "That reminds me, you won't be viewing anything if I don't fix those eyes of yours. Hold on a second…Paul! Paul!" God was yelling out to someone at his house. "Over here…did the Chosen One return yet? No? Okay, thanks." He came back on the line. "That concerns me, Buddy. I wonder what is taking Jesus so long."

"Like you don't know?" I asked. "You are God, aren't you, the one who knows all things?"

"I am, and I do, but I don't follow his every move," God said. "He probably got a flat tire or has broken down again on the side of the road."

"What's he driving?" I asked.

God went into this long explanation about how when Christ returned from the cross, he offered to buy him any car on the market for his troubles, but for some reason, Jesus insists on sporting around in some old rattletrap instead, claiming it keeps him humble.

"Can you imagine," God continued, "your Savior, beating around town in an old Studebaker with fenders flapping in the wind, duct tape holding the bumper on, burning more oil than gas? Makes me look bad, but then maybe that's his way of getting back at me for sending him to Earth in the first place. You know, Buddy, he's still a little pissed about all that."

"I'm sure he is. In fact, according to scriptures, it didn't sound like he was a very happy guy," I said.

"Well, I had to do something, Buddy. Earth was coming apart at the seams. At the time, insider trading was on the rise—cost my son his life, you know—and kings were strutting their stuff like they were involved in creating the big bang. And then you had to have heard about him at the check-cashing center, flipping tables over!"

"Yeah, and I hope we're not going to be making him even madder by asking him to fix my vision. I'd rather spend an eternity in a total blur than upset him any more than he already is," I said, revealing an element of concern.

"No, it's the least he can do," God replied. "Let me try to get him on the two-way. I'll put you back on the speakerphone." (Bleep-bleep) "God to Jesus, do you copy?" (Bleep-bleep) "God to Jesus, come in? He probably won't answer, knows that I…"

(Bleep-bleep) "Yes, Father, I'm in a bad area. You're breaking up."

"Oh, he's so full of it sometimes, Buddy. Acts like there's bad reception in Heaven. I'll turn up the wattage; that'll cut the crap!" (Bleep-bleep) *"Can you hear me now?"*

(Bleep-bleep) "Loud and clear. That's much better. Go ahead," he responded.

(Bleep-bleep) "Jesus Christ, what are you doing? You've been gone for over an hour. The Wild One is back and he needs your assistance."

(Bleep-bleep) "Sorry, Dad, but my car won't start. I left the headlights on. It seems to me that it's probably time for a new battery."

(Bleep-bleep) "Come on, just tell the damned thing to *start* and get back here. Use your God-given powers, Son!"

(Bleep-bleep) "I don't want to. I'm going to wait for Triple-H to show up and give me a jump."

I cut in, "Who…is Triple-H?"

"Heaven's Helping Hands. They offer roadside assistance, but he doesn't need them—he's the Son of God, for Christ's sake. Drives me crazy. The only time he seems to use his power is when he's all jiggered up and wants to impress the ladies!"

"Come on, God," I said, "Jesus is…"

"No, really! If the people on Earth suddenly learned that Jesus was at the liquor store with a dead battery waiting for Triple-H to help him, six billion people would be wiped out from acute laughter."

God gets Jesus on the two-way again. (Bleep-bleep) "All right, then, have it your way, Son. I mean, you being the Savior and all. Come and see me when you get back, and whatever you do, Jesus, don't park that thing in the driveway. It's leaking tranny fluid."

(Bleep-bleep) "Ten-four, Father, over and out."

"Now what, God?" I asked, feeling helpless.

"I don't know. Looks like I have to perform the operation myself if we're to correct that vision..."

"No surgery—I'll be all right!" I exclaimed.

Then God must have sensed my anxiety with the whole idea, and he said, "Settle down, Buddy, I'm only kidding. Is Tucker still around?"

"I don't see him," I said.

"Ah," the Almighty chuckled..."that's funny...let me try something. Close both eyes and repeat after me the words, 'You Rock, God!' Try it now."

"You Rock, God!"

"Open them."

"Wow! That's incredible, God. Way to go."

"Can you see now?" he asked.

"Yes, yes I can, thank you."

"Pretty, isn't it?"

"No, no, actually, I'm not that way, God."

"What!" He seemed surprised. "Tell me what you see. Maybe I did something wrong for once." He laughed, then explained how he likes to have Christ do all of the healing work in Heaven, his being every doctor's dream...or nightmare, depending on how you want to look at it.

I paused for a moment, studying what was before me, and then said to God, "Well, it's white in color, about five and a half feet tall, has red curly hair, and it's wearing a pair of black-rimmed, double-pane glasses, and…"

"Oh! You had me scared there for a second," God remarked. "That's just Tucker. Have him take you down the hall to Life Review, and then get over here as quick as you can."

"Wait, one more thing before you hang up, God."

"What, another miracle, Wilde?"

"Actually, I just wanted to ask if there's any way you could send me back to Earth. I didn't live a perfect life, you know, and I'd do anything to have another shot at going back to make things right."

"Buddy, I'll tell you something. Through God, all things are possible, but don't get your hopes up."

"But I love that child more than anything, God, and you want to deny her and me of that love?"

"Like the song says, Buddy, 'Love is a wonderful thing'—and it is not my desire to withhold it from anyone. However, you're here now, and what you should really focus on at this time is your relationship with me, and the unending love I have for you. But hey, never hurts to talk about it."

"That'd be great! Thanks, God—see you soon."

"If God did not exist, it would be necessary to invent him."

Voltaire – *Letters*

Born Again Christian

We sin no more.

Fill a tall glass with ice. Sprinkle a dash of cinnamon over ice and then add a splash of 7-Up, 6 oz. of carrot juice and 2 oz. of apple juice. Stir well. Garnish with fresh apple wedge.

Crucifixion

It's to die for!

Fill a shaker glass with ice. Add 1½ shots of Grey Goose Vodka, ½ shot of Chambord raspberry liqueur and ½ shot of Triple Sec orange liqueur. Strain and serve in a chilled martini glass.

CHAPTER 4

I Can See!

After hanging up the phone from talking with God, Tucker told me that he had to go answer a page and that I was to wait in bed for his return. With him gone, however, I decided to get up and mosey around, check the place out, see what it had to offer.

Now as one might expect Heaven to be, the décor was very impressive, but there were no windows to speak of, and that seemed rather strange. Then, looking off to my right, I saw the guy who had been making all the gasp-and-gurgle sounds with each breath. He doesn't look well, I thought to myself, and he's probably one of those guys that lived on pizza and smoked like a car fire. I was afraid to get too close, so I hollered out to him from a few feet away, "Hello! Good morning. You awake?" I asked.

"Yes," he responded, all drugged up.

"What are you here for?" I asked.

"Not sure," he said, "but I hurt all over."

"What happened to you?"

"Who knows?" he said with one eye partially open. "Last thing I remember was hearing a loud crack in the sky above me, and then getting thrown up in the air."

"Wow! Sounds as if you were struck by lightning. Too bad, looks like you got messed up."

"I don't (coughing) know what's all wrong with me, but I think it's pretty serious," he said.

"Do you know where you are?" I asked, hoping that maybe he could fill me in on how some things work in Heaven.

"Not really," he said, "I just hope my wife can make her way over here. She's not very good at finding her way around."

"I'm sure she'll manage," I said, trying to comfort him, even though I knew it might take her another fifty years to cross over. "I'm going to take a look around and see what this place has to offer. Maybe we can talk later on, when you're feeling better."

Stepping out the door I turned to the left like I knew the place well and was stopped dead in my tracks. "Holy…!" The hallway stretched for as far as the eye could see, with hundreds and hundreds of glass doorways, but not a soul in sight. Typically, one might expect to see a bunch of doctors and nurses walking around, maybe some empty gurneys, food trays, wheel chairs, monitors, IV stands, bed pans, spent crash carts, a janitor or a mop, perhaps.

"Must be lunch time. I wonder where the cafeteria is. Maybe it's the other way." So I spun around on one heel and was met with two beady blue eyes. It was Tucker.

"Now, Buddy," he questioned, "what are you doing out of bed? Let's go, get back in there."

Sitting back down on the bed, I asked of Tucker, "Another person died?"

"Two of them came back together this time."

"What happened, Tucker?"

"I'd rather not say, Buddy."

"Please? Just tell me what happened, then I'll fully cooperate with you, Tucker. I promise."

He thought for a moment and then said, "Do you swear that if I tell you what happened, Buddy, you'll complete your Life Review without causing any further disturbance?"

"I will."

"Scout's honor?" he asked.

"Certainly, for you, Tucker, by all means."

"Well, I'm not really at liberty to talk about this," he began, "but two females came back, a twenty-nine-year-old woman and her three-month-old daughter. The child died from Sudden Infant Death Syndrome and the mother took her own life because of it. And little does this woman know, she won't be having cocktails with God anytime soon because her name hasn't been added to the guest list yet."

"Wow! That's heavy. Does it happen very often, people killing themselves like that?"

"Suicides are few and far between for me, but I handle about three hundred SIDS cases per year. That's what I specialize in."

"What do you mean, 'handle,' Tucker? What's your relationship to these others, if you're not a doctor?"

"Same as with you. I serve as their spirit guide."

"But three hundred cases a year—why so many?"

"I don't know for sure," he said, "but it's a huge market, very common. Lots of spirits go to Earth only to die a short time later from it."

"Why?" I asked.

"The way I see it, Buddy, most souls go to the physical plane with these big plans for evolution, but know in advance that they'll eventually get bogged down in the density of 'time and space' or the fruitless pleasures of Earth— and then may require a shot of espresso to jack them up again. The death of an infant—any tragedy or major setback in life, for that matter—reawakens their true purpose and usually gets them back on track…but it doesn't always go that way. For some beings it backfires and they never see the light."

"Pardon my expression, Tucker, but you make it sound like human life is a cheap commodity around here, something we consume, then add to the waste stream without ever thinking twice about it."

"You're not too far off, Buddy. Some spirits go through more bodies than they do actual clothes."

"I still don't follow," I said, totally confused.

"Look at it this way," he said. "How can someone go to Earth and practice medicine, if no other spirits are willing to go there and break a leg, or develop heart disease, or get in a bad car wreck?"

"Wow, good point, if that's in fact how it works."

"Trust me," he said, "I've never seen a life-altering event take place on the physical plane outside the process of Divine Agreement."

"Are you saying that this guy next to me actually agreed to get struck by lightning?"

"No, in his case, lightning struck a passing car, which went out of control and then hit him."

"And he chose that as his way to die?" I asked.

"Without a doubt. There are no accidents in life. Let's go, Buddy. We can talk along the way. Out the door and to your right."

We started walking down the hall and I asked Tucker

where he was taking me. "Down to Audio/Digital. It's equipped with the latest, state-of-the-art technology for completing the Life Review," he said.

"Tell me, what will we be doing there, Tucker?"

"You'll be reviewing your entire life, Buddy, from the moment you incarnated to the time you exited your body. I like to look at it as Judgment Day. Somehow God figured out that humans are tougher on themselves than he could ever be, so it works rather well."

"But I already…"

"Don't fight me on this, Buddy. Everyone returning from Earth must do it!"

"But I'm telling you, I already did."

"Don't start," he said.

"Tucker, remember, the motorcycle accident, when I slammed into the tree?"

"I don't recall," he said.

"You don't recall? Get real! It was one of the biggest events in my life! Prior to that I was hell on wheels, tearing up the town—it was a major turning point for me and you don't remember?"

"Please, refresh my memory," he said.

I told him how I'd just turned eighteen, went to a wedding reception driving my motorcycle, got liquored up and was flying down the service road about seventy miles an hour, couldn't make the turn, blacked out, then crashed into the big elm.

"And then?" he asked.

"I reviewed my entire life, Tucker. It flashed by in awesome detail, and nothing was left out. From there I followed a brilliant white light up a dark tunnel, experienced the indescribable love of God, embraced a shadowy figure I thought to be Christ, and was told to go back because my life on Earth wasn't finished yet—then woke up doing cartwheels down the city sidewalk. It was a rush!"

"If what you say is true, Buddy, I must have been preoccupied with something more important at the time."

I stopped and said, "I have a question, Tucker."

"Keep walking, Buddy."

"No, wait! I need to know something right now, and I'm not taking another step until you answer me, and truthfully at that."

"Go ahead," he said, agreeing to let me continue.

"Let me think for a sec…okay. You're a spirit guide, whose job it is to work with and watch over souls that go to Earth, correct?"

"Yes," he responded.

"Earlier you told me that you handle about three hundred SIDS cases a year, and maybe a few suicides or what have you. Are you still with me?"

"I am."

"All right, Tucker, now go back to when I came into Receiving. You were not aware of the fact that I damaged the church with the wrecking ball. And then when I mentioned to you that I already did a Life Review, you didn't know what I was talking about, right?"

"I said that I didn't recall and must have been…"

"Gotcha!"

"What?" he asked.

"You were preoccupied with something more important at the time. That says it all right there!"

"You listen here, Buddy Wilde! I did the very best I could considering what I had to work with. Ever since God called and asked me if I would do him a 'special favor,' my life has been a living hell!"

"What's that got to do with me, Tucker?"

"Everything! God said that he had a struggling soul very dear to him that needed a spirit guide to do Earth and asked if I would help out. Had I known then what I know now, I would have gone out on sick leave."

"And what do you know now that you didn't know then, Tucker—that you would need to pay close attention to me, like a spirit guide should?"

"No! That it would be 'you' whom I would be asked to guide," he said.

"What's so terribly bad about that?" I asked. "I mean, how is it that I somehow made your life this living hell? You could have saved us both a lot of trouble if you had just done your job instead of playing Mr. Big-Shot over in Receiving. And then, why did you agree to take the assignment in the first place if you knew it was me you'd be guiding?"

Tucker looked down at the floor, and then back up again. "I didn't. God tricked me," he said.

"Oh go on. He wouldn't do that," I said. "I'm sure that if the Almighty wants anyone to do something around here, all he has to do is ask."

"You don't know God, Buddy!"

"Really…?" I questioned him, hoping he would give me a truckload on God, some real insider information I could use later if need be.

"Not at all! If you want my honest opinion," Tucker said, "I think God views the entire universe as one big cocktail party."

"You know," I added, "there does seem to be some association to alcohol with everything around here. Does he have a problem I should know about?"

"I can't be the judge of that," Tucker replied.

"Has anyone ever tried intervention?"

"Jesus did, but…well, God blew a fuse."

"People do that," I said. "Has something to do with deep-seated anger. But tell me this, Tucker, how is it that you think God screwed you over so bad by asking you to be my spirit guide?"

"Doesn't matter. The damage is already done."

"No, if this involves me, I want to hear it!"

Tucker began walking. "It all started some years ago when God called Receiving and asked me to join him for a cocktail at his house after work. He knows I don't drink, but he was…"

"Three gurneys to the morgue?" I offered.

"Exactly—or at least he acted like it. When I walked in, he was getting out of his favorite recliner and stumbled over to the kitchen table. I was afraid to sit down. The place was a complete disaster from the night before—empty booze bottles everywhere, ashtrays filled to the brim, women's underwear hanging from the chandelier, food still out that should have been put away. Anyhow, he unfolded this sheet of paper and tossed it to me—it was an Application to Do Earth—then asked if I would help him out. So I began reading it and he offered to fix me a Nazarene, but I don't drink…"

"A Nazarene?" I said, interrupting.

"God's favorite martini," he said. "Anyway, God gave me the application, which was stained so heavily with Irish Cream and coffee I could barely read it. The name of the applicant was smeared beyond recognition. Looked like he had carried it around in his back pocket for a few years. With that, just when I was about to ask him the subject's name, he said that he was feeling wheezy, and that I should go because the soul on the application in question was cleared for takeoff earlier in the day and had already incarnated to Earth."

"Did he throw up?" I asked.

"No! He wasn't even drunk. It was all an act."

"An act? What about him stumbling around, the empty booze bottles, and the underwear?"

"They were props," Tucker said, "had to be! He actually tricked me into being your spirit guide."

"Can he hear us talking right now?" I asked.

"He could, but with all the goings-on of Earth, he usually keeps Heaven on mute during business hours."

I took a moment to formulate my next question and asked, "So you believe that God set you up. What did you do then?"

"I went over to Records," he said, "hoping to pull the master file and learn more about the subject's previous Earth experiences. Askmee, the head record keeper, figured out it was probably your application, but when she searched for your file, it came back 'no records found'— yet it wouldn't have mattered anyway. I'm sure it would have been full of lies, just like the application you filled out."

"Wait just a second, Tucker! If there's one thing I pride myself on, it's in telling the truth."

"We're here, Buddy. Let's go inside."

Not liking what Tucker had just implied, I leaned against the wall and dropped to the floor.

"Get up!" he said.

"Nope! I don't think so."

"But you promised to fully cooperate with me!"

"Well, I might break a promise now and then, maybe even stretch the truth, but I don't fill other people with lies. I'm not going any farther until…"

"I've got it right here. I'll read it to you." he said.

Tucker took a deep breath and then began, "When asked to state your Purpose for Incarnation, and to give a detailed plan to accomplish your mission, you wrote: 'In order that I may clear up some old karmic debt, I want to be born and left for dead in a poor, third-world country landfill only to experience severe starvation and sickness the first three years of my life before being adopted by an affluent American family—where I am critically injured after getting run over in front of school by our nanny, just prior to being diagnosed with terminal bone cancer the following Christmas—wherein I spend the next five years in and out of hospitals battling my disease, to which I lose my life.'"

"Wow! I'm impressed, but I don't think bone cancer patients live that long, Tucker."

"Then why didn't you consider that before you wrote it? Now please get up, Buddy."

"You are an Angel.
Beware of those who collect feathers."

The author received this message
in a fortune cookie at a Chinese restaurant.

Second Coming

Still waiting…

Fill an old-fashioned glass with ice. Add 1 oz. of gin and 1½ shots of peach schnapps. Top with cranberry juice. Garnish with an orange slice and a cherry.

Burning Bush

Need a light?

Fill a shaker glass with ice. Add 2 drops of dry vermouth, 1 shot of vodka, and 1 shot of peppered vodka. Shake well and then strain into a chilled martini glass. Garnish with a jalapeno-stuffed olive.

CHAPTER 5
Life Review

Opening the door to Life Review, Tucker pointed me to a sitting area in front of a big-screen TV.

Walking inside, the first thing I noticed was a hand-carved wood bar that stretched across the entire back wall. "How cool...look at that, Tucker! I've been in some of the best saloons in the world and have never seen anything like this before. And these lounge chairs, they would cost a fortune back on Earth. Where's the leather from?" Must be imported, I thought. "And the decorating, it's fabulous," I said, taking in a panoramic view of the entire room. "Who's the talented one behind all of this?"

"Two lady friends of Sam," he answered.

"Wow, I must say, Tucker, they have fine taste. But tell me, is their flair for interior design any reflection of what they might look like?"

"Buddy, you wouldn't believe it," he continued. "We're talking about two of the finest women in Heaven."

"Really, what're their names?" I asked.

"Catchme and Doome." Tucker's face lit up.

"What?" I thought he was joking.

"Catchme and Doome. They're twins, Buddy."

"You've got to be kidding. What do they look like? I have to know."

"As I said, two of the finest women in Heaven," Tucker replied.

"Are they around here now?" I asked.

"No, but you can meet them sometime after you finish up here with me. They both dance in the evening over at a gentleman's club called Behinds. Sam hangs out there a lot and I'm sure that he'll be delighted to take you there. You need to sit down now." I began thinking to myself that a life in Heaven might not be so bad after all.

"Wait," I said to Tucker, "are you telling me they have strip clubs in Heaven?" I walked over toward the bar to get a closer look at it.

"We have everything you could ever imagine, Buddy," he said. "Let's begin."

I went over and took a high-back leather chair next to Tucker in front of a big-screen TV and he handed me a little package of tissues, saying, "Here, Buddy, you'll need these."

"What for?" I asked.

"To dry your eyes."

"My eyes are fine. Don't worry about me."

"They won't be when you're done with this, Buddy. No one has ever completed a Life Review without shedding at least a few tears."

Tucker picked up the remote, clicked the Play button and the program began:

"Welcome to 'This Was Your Life.' My name is God and I'll be hosting the show."

The screen filled with snow and diagonal lines. "Some state-of-the-art technology you have here, Tucker."

He laughed and then said to me, "Pay attention, Buddy. The filming or photography of God's face is strictly prohibited."

The program continued with the voice of God:

"Today we'll take a look back in time and review every second of your experience on the physical plane— your entire life was all caught on tape to ensure accuracy (nude photos of every woman I ever slept with flashed across the screen) *from the day you incarnated to the moment your soul left its body. But first, before I forget, let's have a word from our sponsor."*

A scantily dressed, sexy brunette in her early thirties came on the big screen with a seductive voice and said: *"Hey, stranger, feeling tired and bored with the spirit world yet? How would you like to have a little fun in your life... Ewww? Then bust out of your comfort zone and go down where the action is—planet Earth!*

"Pick up the phone and call me, Love. If you do, you'll receive a free pass to any exciting adventure you can dream of. Just choose a life purpose or theme, anything you want, and we'll not only make all the necessary arrangements, but we'll also get you there free of charge. (She was on a roll.)

"Just imagine the possibilities—you could be a movie star, a billionaire, a president, or intern—there's over one million roles to choose from.

"Think about it, guys! Where else in the cosmos can you experience the birth of a newborn, the death of a loved one, the marriage of lovers, or a real knock-down-drag-out divorce?

"In addition, planet Earth also offers live volcanoes, earthquakes, tornados and floods—so what are you waiting for?

"But stop! That's not all. If you pick up the phone and call this instant, we'll even throw in a soul-mate that you can play hide-and-seek with for the next thirty years. How fun!

"Now don't delay, guys, because you know what they say—'There's no place in Heaven like Earth.' Call Back-U-Go Travel—today!"

The screen turned back to snow and diagonal lines again. Then I asked Tucker, "What in the world was that all about? Unbelievable."

"Ah, God runs these commercials during Life Review. He's worried that if conditions on Earth get any worse, people will stop reincarnating and Heaven will experience overcrowding, so he likes to keep cycling returning spirits back to Earth again using these messages."

"Then why did he cut my life short?" I had to ask. "I'm just taking up space here. I could be with my family right now. Makes no sense to me whatsoever."

"I can't answer that, Buddy. Shhh!"

The voice of God came back on to offer some instructions for viewing the program. He began…

"If at any time you need to use the bathroom, ask your spirit guide to stop the program and return to it when you are finished. Should you get hungry, break for lunch anytime you like, and if you happen to get thirsty, there's beer, behind the bar. Help yourself."

"That's just what I wanted to hear, Tucker. Stop the program!"

"It hasn't even begun yet, Buddy!"

"I don't care. I want a beer."

"But you should wait until the Review is over."

"Hey, if God said there's beer behind the bar and to help myself, I'm going for it. I'll be right with you." I hurried over there. "Why don't you order out for some food, Tucker. I don't like to drink on an empty stomach...What do we have here? White Lite, on tap. Is it any good?" I asked Tucker.

"I don't know, but the angels drink it like there's no eternity," he said, dialing the phone to order a pizza.

"Why not," I said, "it's probably less filling. Mind if I drink out of a pitcher?"

"Yes, I mind, Buddy. I don't want you getting drunk. Just pour yourself a small glass and quit playing around back there."

"Care to join me, Tucker?"

"Believe me, I'd like to tip a few right about now, but I never drink on the job."

Since God didn't specifically mention or limit quantity, I began filling a large mug and noticed a book on the counter. I picked it up. *Heavenly Drinks—The Official Bartender's Guide to Making Cocktails That Are Out of This World.*

I cracked it open. "Ah...listen to this, Tucker. 'The Crucifixion.' Says here, 'It's to die for!' How cool is that? And check this out. It gives recipes for a 'Bible Thumper,' 'Jehovah's Witness'—ah, that's funny—'Doubting Thomas,' 'Nazarene,' 'Act of God,' 'Wing and a Prayer'—that sounds good about now. Where can I get a copy of this?" I asked.

Tucker came to get me out from behind the bar, pulling me by the arm. "At the bookstore, when we are finished, Buddy."

"Easy, boss! You're going to make me spill!"

Tucker led me over to my chair and hit the Play button. I took a pull off of my beer.

"What the hell's that?" I yelped, staring at an ungodly sight on the TV.

"Prenatal, Buddy. That's what you looked like inside your mother's womb," he said.

"No, Tucker, I'm talking about all those squiggly lines of white and brown stuff?"

"Oh, that. Oatmeal and coffee, Buddy. She practically lived on it."

"Gross! Hit fast-forward. I don't want to watch that. Yuk!"

"Look, Buddy, here's the part where you are actually born into the world."

"Ah...that had to hurt," I said. "God should really reconsider redesigning the...hold on, what's this guy doing grabbing me by the ankles like that and smacking me on the backside?" I couldn't believe what I was seeing. "That's child abuse!"

"No, to make you cry," Tucker said. "Helps to make you take your first breath."

"Like hell! All's that did was piss me off! It's no wonder why people go through life mad at the world—you get your ass kicked on the way in, as well as on the way out, not to mention all the beating we experience in between." I took another swig of beer. "This ain't bad stuff, Tucker, and it's priced right."

He laughed, "Pay attention, Buddy." The program continued.

When the next scene came on, Tucker spoke as if he was saddened with having to see me go through this particular event in life. There I was, being expelled from Catholic school in the fourth grade. Tucker said in a soft voice, "Awe, that's too bad, you weren't a very well-liked student there, Buddy."

"No shit. Look at my knuckles. They're ready to bleed, for Christ's sake! I would have liked to shove one of those splintered rulers up someone's…"

"Be nice," Tucker cut in, wanting to somehow protect me from my own anger.

"That's easy for you to say, but I'll bet you never had a nun make you sit under a desk with her at it wherein all you smelt for three hours was feet and seat—she probably didn't have a bath in six months, Tucker." He smiled, trying not to focus on the visual I had planted in his mind.

The program continued. A few minutes went by, and then Tucker sat up.

"I don't remember this part of your life, Buddy. Oh, my lord, lucky you didn't get killed!"

"No thanks to you," I said. "One would venture to believe that anytime there's two young kids playing with gasoline that could explode and burn their face off, a good spirit guide might be around to help put the fire out—wouldn't you say?"

"I must have been in conference that day," he said, trying to think back. "Oh, doesn't matter anyway. Sidekick takes care of all that hands-on stuff, so you were covered, Buddy."

"Sidekick, who's that?" I asked.

"Ah, I'm sorry, Buddy, I completely forgot. Sidekick is your guardian angel. I was going to introduce you to him in Receiving, but he went off the clock the moment you crossed over." Tucker then went on to tell me how I'd forever be indebted to this Sidekick character for having saved my skin from serious injury and death on numerous occasions.

The program was interrupted by another commercial from Back-U-Go Travel, and that same fine-looking specimen who did the voice-over earlier appeared on the screen, but she had dyed her hair blonde.

"Hey guys, feeling lucky—Meow? How would you like to die in the arms of a beautiful lover like me?

"Well, too bad, you can't do it here—no one dies in Heaven. But you can on planet Earth!

"That's right! The physical plane offers thousands of ways to die, more ways than you can shake a stick at. Pick a way to die, any way, and we'll arrange it for you, right down to the moment of your last breath.

"Just picture yourself, dying of a massive heart attack after spending two hours with a babe like me, or of a flesh-eating disease when you walk out the door. However you want to 'go,' we can accommodate most any cause of death.

"What—still undecided? Let me tempt you with this. Sign up now and you may qualify for our new Litigation Special—it could leave your loved ones set for life. That's right! Choose a cause of death that warrants a good lawsuit, and they'll have it made in the shade.

"But in telling you all this, I must also read you the fine print." (She rattled off the legal disclaimer.) *'Compensation for damages are not guaranteed, individual results may vary, and attorney fees will apply.'*

"Now pick up the phone, guys, and call Back-U-Go Travel today!"

"Jesus Lord! What is with this place, Tucker? Why in the world would anyone want to go to Earth and die in the arms of a whore, or of a flesh-eating disease? I've never heard of anything so outrageous! Who's the sick individual that writes these ads?" I asked, demanding to know.

"God," Tucker replied.

"No...way!" I exclaimed.

"Like I said, Buddy, you don't know the Almighty. And he's not sick."

"Then he must be on something," I shouted.

"Shhh!" Tucker said.

The voice of God began, but then there was a knock at the door and it opened. A man wearing a Dominos-like uniform walked in, acknowledged our presence with a nod and then said, "Hi, Large Special, hold the cheese."

Tucker instructed him to set it down on the coffee table in front of us and then picked up the remote to stop the program. The pizza delivery guy left the room and I sat there looking at Tucker, totally amazed.

Tucker opened the box and told me to dig in. I, however, just sat there staring at him.

"What?" Tucker asked. "You don't like pizza, Buddy?" There was dead silence, then he spoke again, "Is there something wrong, Buddy?"

"Are you out of your mind," I asked him, "ordering a pizza with no cheese?"

He replied with half a piece of it in his mouth, "It'll clog your arteries."

"Who cares, Tucker, they're my arteries and I happen to like cheese! Besides, I'm already dead, so how is it that a little extra cholesterol is going to do me any further harm?" Tucker stuffed another piece in his mouth, ignoring my plea for cheese.

"Okay," I said, getting up from my chair, "this calls for another beer, maybe two—one to prepare my mind for eating something you'd find on the side of the road, and another to wash it down."

Tucker objected to my drinking anything more with alcohol in it while we were still in Life Review. "Have some bottled holy water instead, Buddy. We're not even halfway through the program yet," he said, chomping on a piece of the thick crust.

"Holy water, my ass! It's gonna take something mind-altering to even get a piece of that sorry-looking stuff anywhere near my lips." I walked behind the bar and started to pour a mug of White Lite. As it was filling, a thought came to me and I said to Tucker, half-serious, "You know, something tells me that Heaven isn't going to be big enough for the two of us, Tucker, so maybe we should just get God on the phone and tell him to call it off and send me back to my life on Earth."

"He won't do it, Buddy."

"Great! Then I'm left with no other choice than to sneak out of here when no one is looking."

Tucker glanced over to me and remarked, "No one has ever gone back to Earth without God knowing about it, Buddy."

"There's always a first time for everything, Tucker, and if I should happen to come across even the smallest opening that leads out of here, I'll be gone like a thief in the night."

"Fat chance," Tucker said, wiping his mouth.

"Hey, people leave here every day, right? I'll just wait for the Almighty to get good and hammered—like it sounded he was doing today, when I talked with him on the phone—fall in line when they're loading up the shuttle for Earth, stick an in-flight magazine over my face and wait for it to land," I said, sitting down in front of the cheeseless pizza.

Tucker laughed, picking up the remote, "Let's see if we can finish Life Review without any further interruptions, Buddy." He pressed Play and the program picked up where we had left off.

"Look, Tucker, my first true love, turn it up—she was the only woman I'd ever gone out with who acted like a lady in public and a devil in bed. Are you enjoying this?" I asked.

"Buddy, I must say—I'm not amused, but am amazed, with the terminology you use to describe such a sacred act, much less a creation of God."

"Oh, say whatever you want, Tucker. But don't forget, you're sitting here watching me make mad, passionate love to this hot babe and you haven't blinked an eye." He remained silent as the memories of days gone by flashed across the TV.

Tucker spoke, "Here's an admirable moment in your life, Buddy."

On the screen I was shown smoking a joint on the front steps at high school when the principal quietly walked up from behind, put his hand on my shoulder and asked me how my day was going. I heard myself say to the principal, "Not good!" But in reality, I was having a great day until he entered the picture.

"I'll have you know, Tucker, that was a cause I consciously set in motion."

"What—to get suspended from school, Buddy?"

"No, to get kicked out! And it worked to my advantage. I didn't graduate, but I did become a successful businessman." The next scene came on.

"Tucker! Here it is, watch this, since you couldn't be there to witness this in person." The motorcycle accident that nearly cost me my life began to play. "Check it out, Tucker. There I am having the time of my life at the wedding reception, drinking and carrying on with friends...now I'm getting on my bike. Listen to that thing—I ran racing fuel in it. Vroom, vroom! Now I'm getting on the highway, taking the exit ramp, crossing the bridge, down the hill, here comes the curve—wham! Look at that thing come apart—holy shit!"

Now here's where my life flashes, in complete detail, every spec of it, just like I told you back in Receiving. Now do you believe me, Tucker?"

"Buddy, it's not that I didn't believe you. I just didn't recall this ever happening to you," he responded.

In the scene that followed, Tucker started laughing and clapped his hands together. "This has got to be the funniest thing I've ever seen you do, Buddy!" There I was, shown going up on the Internet, becoming an ordained minister in under five minutes, and Tucker couldn't get over it. His feet even came off the floor as he leaned back in his chair, cracking up.

"Are you knocking my ministry, Tucker?"

"What ministry, Buddy? The Unbridled Church of Wannabe Saints—you call that a ministry, serving free Bloody Marys and Screwdrivers on Sunday mornings to draw people in and talk about God?" He continued, insulting me further. "You have no idea how many laughs that got back here."

"What?" I asked.

"Are you kidding me—every hospital in Heaven filled up with spirits experiencing severe respiratory problems—they were laughing so hard that they couldn't catch their breath."

"That's not funny, Tucker. I had the best intentions and a pure heart when I founded that organization, and it would have been a huge success and helped many people had God not called me back." Another commercial came on.

"Hey, guys, me again. (The former brunette who died her hair blonde now appeared with it colored red.) *Why haven't you called? I'm waiting. Which one of you handsome studs is it going to be tonight?* (Her next statement made my blood boil.)

"You boneheads! What were you thinking? You can't get laid in Heaven, Nooooooooooooo!

"The only place to do that is on planet Earth. So what are you hanging around for? Gawk all you want, but it's not happening here, mister—because we need you little darlings doing it back on Earth so that incarnating spirits will have a body to occupy.

"Now try as you might, guys, but you'll see. Your pent-up sexual energy will send you hurling back to Earth— guaranteed!

"Still don't believe me? Ask around. Then pick up the phone and call Back-U-Go Travel."

I stood up from my chair, totally pissed. "Okay, that's it, Tucker! I can't take it any more. Tell me the honest-to-

God truth: Is it this place that's fucked up, or am I just losing my mind?"

"That's how it works here, Buddy."

"Don't tell me that! I'm stuck in this hell hole for what might be forever and even if I wanted to have sex, I'm out of luck?"

"I don't make the rules, Buddy."

"Enough," I screamed. "Shut this goddamned thing off! I'm having another beer and I want out of Heaven—now! Not after I finish Life Review, not even after I meet the Almighty, I want out *now!* Do you hear me, Tucker?" He just stood there looking at me, like a deer caught in the headlights.

I continued, "What a joke! This is worse than any acid trip I've ever been on. I can't believe this shit. First I die of a freak medical condition, then I wake up in Heaven with a spirit guide that acts like he's the Surgeon General. Then I find out God's a real piece of work, Jesus drives a car he couldn't get a leper to ride in, and Sam Kinison is here and hangs out at a strip club in Heaven—what could be next?"

I got up, ready to blow another artery, and walked toward the bar. Tucker stopped the program and then the room filled with the Almighty's angry voice over the loudspeaker: "Turn that back on and sit down!"

I was livid, so I shouted back, "Go play with your deranged self!"

Then, the lights in the room began to flicker as Tucker fumbled with the remote.

"I said turn it back on!" God yelled again.

"Go fuck yourself!" I was hot!

Tucker panicked. "I can't get it to turn on!"

Then God said with a thundering tone, "Here, let me do it, Tucker." The big-screen TV lifted about six feet off the ground and then slammed to the floor.

"Good going, asshole, you just broke the damned thing into a million pieces," I yelled.

From there, bottles of booze from behind the bar started flying around the room.

"You don't scare me, you twisted son of a bitch!" I shouted.

Then plaster began falling from the ceiling. Tucker ran for cover into the adjoining bathroom. It looked like the thing to do, so I followed.

"Get a life, you no-good prick!" I screamed to God, running across the room.

Next, the whole building started bucking back and forth like a wild-bull ride.

"Stick the universe up your ass, motherfucker, planets and all!"

The roof trusses cracked and fell in where we had been sitting. Tucker begged me to stop.

"Mass murderer!" I yelled to God.

The chair I was sitting on earlier lifted up on its own and flew across the room at eye level, getting wedged in the bathroom doorjamb.

"You missed, fuckhead! Try again."

I no more than said that and a bolt of lightning cracked in the open sky, and rain came pouring in.

"Where's the materials to build an ark, you wicked, unforgiving bastard!"

A ball of fire shot in through the open roof.

"You forgot the brimstone, idiot! Let's see what you have for nuclear bombs!" I hollered.

And then as quick as it started, it was over. The rain that fell in helped to knock the dust down. I looked out from beneath the recliner stuck in the doorway. The place resembled a war zone.

I shouted to God, "I'm not cleaning this up! Get your fuckin' maid over here to do it—and you'd better send a carpenter to fix the roof!"

Having been so engaged with God's fury, I forgot about Tucker. By this time he had managed to squeeze his whole body underneath the bathroom vanity, but he hadn't been able to shut the door.

"Better stay in there, Tucker. I got a feeling God's on his way over here to mess you up."

"Me? What did I do, Buddy?"

"You stopped the program and then wouldn't turn it back on when he told you to, and I don't think he goes for that shit."

Tucker wanted to argue that it was me who pissed off the pope, but I ignored him, making my way out of the bathroom to assess the damage, and then the phone rang.

"I'll get it, Tucker," I said, almost out of breath. "It might be the landlord wondering what in the hell we are doing up here."

I located the phone and then answered it, "Life Review, Buddy Wilde speaking."

"This is God, Buddy. Was that wild or what?"

"Yeah, that was pretty wild. Are you done trying to kill me yet?" I said, still breathing hard.

"I haven't had that much fun in ages. I'm not kidding! You keep on competing with me over who's the craziest son of a bitch in the universe and I'll never let you go back—I love it!"

"You can't imprison me here forever, God. So you might just as well give it up and let me go back to Earth."

"Not yet, Buddy. Hang around for a while. We've got all the time in the world. Please listen: not...yet."

"If not now, when?" I asked, wanting a specific time and date.

"I don't know, but everything has its season, Buddy, and it's just not your time. Besides, people are starting to file in for the big party tonight. I want you to come over and have a few cocktails with me."

"Are you serious, even after all we have just been through?"

"Of course! That was nothing," he said.

"Hang on," I said with my knees still shaking, "let me think about this for a second." I took a deep breath. "Would you mind if I took a shower first, maybe find something else to wear?"

"Fine," God said, "have Tucker bring you down to Hospitality, where you can get cleaned up. Then he can walk you over to my house. Be here by seven."

"What about finishing my Life Review?" I asked.

"Don't worry about it. Do it some other time," he said.

"Okay, but I think Tucker is stuck under the sink."

"Well, I really hate to see you wreck anything, but tear it apart if you have to, Buddy."

"You won't get mad, God?"

"I'll look the other way. Talk with you soon."

Hanging up the phone, I went over to the bathroom. "Tucker, you can come out now."

"I can't, I'm stuck." He sounded worried.

"Oh, here, let me help you. I'm going to use one of these roof boards and smash the marble top."

"No, don't, Buddy! Just pull my leg out—it's pinned. Then I can free myself."

"All right, hang on… (Whack!) That's better, now just stand up and brush yourself off."

"Wilde!" he screamed. It was the first time I'd seen Tucker get mad.

"What? I got you out, didn't I?"

Climbing out of the vanity, he went into the other room. "Oh, my God, look at this place. It's a total disaster! I've never seen him do that before."

"I know, and he loved every minute of it, Tucker. I'm glad the Almighty has a good sense of humor. Otherwise I might be in trouble," I said.

"So, what did God say on the telephone, Buddy?"

"Ah…he wants me to grab another beer, go down to Hospitality and draw a hot bath, while you go out and find me a nice black tux to wear to the party."

"God is the greatest democrat the world knows, for He leaves us 'unfettered' to make our own choice between evil and good."

Mohandas K. Gandhi
Statements on the Nature of God,
published in *Young India*

Ten Commandments

Thou shalt not...but do it anyway!

Fill a tall glass with ice. Then add 1 shot of Southern Comfort, 1 shot of Malibu Rum, 1 oz. of orange juice and 2 oz. of cranberry juice. Garnish with a twist of orange.

Noah's Ark

Pour your shots 2 X 2

Fill a pitcher with ice and then add:
4 oz. spiced rum
2 oz. citrus vodka
4 oz. pineapple juice
4 oz. orange juice
4 oz. 7-Up
Add a splash of grenadine for color. Stir well and pour into tall glasses. Serves 4 to 6.

CHAPTER 6

Those Pearly Gates

Having it out in a fire fight with God is quite the experience; being invited over to his house for cocktails is another. I didn't know what to expect—one part of me was totally excited, the other, terrified! Only time would tell where this would lead.

"How do I look, Tucker?"

"Like a million bucks," he said. "God will be impressed, Buddy."

"Honestly?" I asked my spirit guide.

"You haven't a thing to worry about," he said.

"Let's move, then—can't be late. I want to go over there and have a cocktail with God, maybe even apologize for my earlier behavior. I don't know what came over me. And by the way, Tucker, I should probably tell you that I'm sorry as well for putting you through hell, both when I first came into Receiving, and during Life Review. I just wasn't ready for any of this stuff yet."

"I understand, Buddy, and thanks. But it goes with the job," he said.

As we reached the end of the hall, Tucker opened a door and we walked outside for the first time. I was struck with the most beautiful landscape I had ever seen.

"Look at them pearly gates, Tucker. Don't tell me they're made of plastic."

"Real pearls. I forget how many, but it's in the tens of thousands," he said.

"And those houses on the hillside—looks similar to Vermont. No billboards or pollution. I like it."

"See God's house over there, Buddy," Tucker pointed off to my left.

"That's not a house—it's a city!"

"Millions of square feet. You can actually get lost in there," he said.

"What all's in it?" I asked.

"Everything you could think of, Buddy. Dozens of night clubs, a food court, fancy restaurants, duty-free shops, a theme park, supermarket, theaters, you name it."

"How many bedrooms, Tucker?"

"Several hundred, and they all have Jacuzzis with fully stocked wet bars in them."

"Are you trying to get rid of me, Tucker?"

"Actually, I do need to go back to Receiving for a while and then get cleaned up so I can join you at the party."

We walked side-by-side up the driveway in silence, my mind preoccupied with thoughts of meeting God. Would he actually greet me with open arms? Or was I about to be judged to death for all the loveless acts I had committed in my life, and then cast into outer darkness for an eternity? We neared the entry to God's house.

"Thanks, Tucker. I owe you one."

"Ring the door bell, Buddy. I'll see you later," he

said, turning away to walk back down the driveway.

I pushed the button and waited, but no one came. Should I ring it again, I wondered? I might piss off the butler, but someone has to let me in. Just then it opened.

"Jesus Christ! What are you doing answering the door?" I was shocked.

"Come in, Buddy, come in. Wow! We've been expecting you."

"Get him a drink," a scrappy voice yelled out from nowhere.

"Oh! Don't tell, Jesus—let me guess. Is that you, God? I'd recognize that voice anywhere."

"It's me, Buddy!"

"But where…are you invisible or what? I can't see you."

"Right here, my friend." God jumped out from behind the door, wearing a long white robe trimmed in gold. "Put 'em up, Wilde, let's go another round." He started shadowboxing, throwing jabs in my direction.

"Not in the house," I said, trying to avoid another confrontation with the Almighty.

"How about another fire fight, then, like over in Life Review? We'll go out back, though," he said, "where there's more room to wreck stuff."

"Some other time, God, but I will take a drink."

"Then pour the champagne, Son. Shit," he said, "it's been over thirty years, Wilde—good to see you again."

Jesus cut in, "Yeah, get this, Buddy, Father hasn't quit laughing since you came back to Heaven. Hopefully you'll incarnate soon," he said.

God came over, I thought to give me a big hug, but it turned out to be a headlock. Then he wrestled me to the

floor saying, "I'm so happy to have you back, Wilde—yes!"
Jesus spoke. "He knows, Father, he knows. Now get off of him, for Heaven's sake."

God let me up and straightened out his robe. "I didn't wrinkle your tux, did I?"

"I'm fine, God," I said, brushing myself off.

Jesus handed us each a glass of the sparkling wine and proposed a toast. "To our Father, for creating the one-and-only Buddy Wilde." Jesus and I each took a drink.

God, on the other hand, drank his in one gulp, then said to me, "Pound it down, Wilde, go-go-go—there's more where that came from!"

Out of shear joy that it seemed I'd somehow been spared from an eternity in Hell, I followed his lead. "Pour us another one for the road, Son," the Almighty ordered. I was taken aback with the carefreeness of God, and his party-animal-like attitude.

"I hope you're ready for this, Wilde...there's two hundred people here waiting to see you and they all want to buy you a drink." Turning toward Jesus, God asked him, "Do you think he can handle it, Son?"

"Only time will tell, Father," Jesus said, knowing full well that that much alcohol would cause me to drown in my own vomit early on.

"Let's blow. We'll take Greased Lightning. You drive, Son."

"Greased Lightning? What's that?" I asked Jesus.

"Oh, just one of Dad's toys." Jesus walked me over to a street rod of a golf cart, with wheelie bars and side pipes. "She'll do zero to sixty in a heartbeat, Buddy."

"Through the house?" I asked God.

"Why not? Everything's insured," he said.

We all jumped into God's deathtrap. I sat next to the

Almighty in the back seat; Jesus got behind the wheel and
hit the ignition. Vroom, vroom! It sounded like a top fuel
dragster, rough idle and all.

"I can't find my seatbelt," I said to God.

"Don't worry about it, Wilde. You can't die in
Heaven," he replied.

"Are you sure?" I said, seeking reassurance.

"No one has yet. Put her down, Son!"

The tires squealed and we were off. It was like we
were driving through the Mall of America, after-hours, at a
high rate of speed, flying by storefronts and specialty shops.

"I use this to check the mail, Wilde. My son loves
it." God hollered up to Jesus, poking fun at him, "Beats
walking, wouldn't you say, Jesus?"

"If you only knew," Jesus answered, swerving from
side to side to demonstrate his joy.

"So what do you think of Heaven?" God asked me,
probably expecting I'd say I love it.

"It's not bad," I said, "that is, if you just came back,
leaving a body behind that was crawling with cancer."

"You're not impressed?" He looked surprised.

"It's nice, God, really is. I just wasn't ready to leave
my life on Earth yet. I miss my daughter more than you'll
ever know. It tears my heart out just thinking about her." I
thought back to a promise I had made to her just a few days
prior to being struck with the deadly ruptured aneurysm.

"Hey, hey, Buddy," God said, "have a few drinks,
check out some of the sites, hang out with me for a while
and you'll forget all about it. And besides, in Heaven time
flies, so your daughter will be with you before you know
it," he said.

"That's all fine and dandy, God, but I made her a
promise the other day that I'll never be able to keep—that

bugs me more than anything."

"I understand, Buddy. Most spirits returning from the physical plane leave there with unfinished business, so what you are telling me isn't anything I haven't heard before. Most everyone reacts the same way."

"Yeah, but they probably weren't yanked out of their life in the best part of it, like I was. You could not have timed this any worse," I said.

"Listen, Buddy, according to the beliefs of human beings, there is no good time to cross over. But for me, any time is a good time."

"A 'good time,' as in 'fun,' God? Are you insane, or what?" I was thinking to myself, "Here we go again—where can I hide out this time?"

"No," God said, "and it's not like I wake up each day and ask myself, 'Who can I pluck out of the world today?' It doesn't work that way. People are the ones who pick the day they'll die, and how it will happen. I have nothing to do with that."

Even though I disagreed with God, believing that I should still be alive on Earth trying to get my crazy life straightened out, I bit my tongue. After all, God could have killed me during Life Review had he wanted to, so I just kept my mouth shut.

"Every day,
people are straying
away from the church
and going back to God."

Lenny Bruce

Guardian Angel

No sleeping on the job.

In a coffee mug, add 1 shot of Bailey's Irish Cream, ½ shot of Amaretto liqueur, ½ shot of Frangelico hazelnut liqueur. Then fill with freshly brewed coffee. Cap with whipped cream. Lightly sprinkle cinnamon and sugar on top.

Blessed Sacramenthe

The answer to your prayers.

In an old-fashioned glass with ice, mix 2 shots of bourbon with 1 shot of crème de menthe.

CHAPTER 7

Welcome Home!

With the three of us climbing out of God's custom golf cart in front of what appeared to be a swanky night club, Jesus opened a large French door and gestured with his hand for me to follow him into a dark room, with the Almighty close behind. Then the lights went on and two hundred people stood up and cheered. God stepped forward and announced: "Ladies and gentlemen, Buddy Wilde. Hit it, Sam!" The crowd cheered again. Jimmy Hendrix, Stevie Ray Vaughan and comedian Sam Kinison took off on the electric guitars playing *Born to Be Wild*, with Janis Joplin on vocals. Everyone in the audience sang along.

When the song was over, God said, "Up to the bar, Wilde, I'm buying. Three Nazarenes, Son." He signaled Jesus to mix the drinks.

"Crucified or Resurrected, Father?"

"Resurrected, Son."

"Martinis?" I asked God.

"That's right, Wilde, my favorite. And Jesus likes it when I order them; makes him feel special." We both bellied up to the bar.

"I suppose it does, God. Tell me, though, who're the two babes at the end of the bar?"

"Oh, that's Catchme and Doome, friends of Sam. They handle all my interior design by day and dance over in Matter Ville at night. Hi, girls."

"My lord!" I was hoping the Almighty would invite them over to give us a little show.

"I don't make them any finer than what you see right there," God said, "but don't be fooled by good looks alone. They're both a couple of smart cookies."

"Yeah, but you know, God, what good does it do to be drop-dead gorgeous if you can't have sex in Heaven?"

"Don't believe everything you hear, Buddy." God took a big drink of the martini.

I protested. "Well, according to Tucker, you wrote all those ads that aired during Life Review. It sounded to me as if a guy couldn't get lucky around here, even if his life depended on it."

"Then sue me for false advertising," he said.

"So it's not true?" I asked God.

"Correct, but there's a reason for it."

Jesus put the martinis in front of us and offered a toast: "To our Father, for not turning the Wild One back into stardust during Life Review."

"Thanks, Son."

God continued, "Here's the problem. Everyday I'm faced with hundreds of guys who die and come back from Earth hoping to finally meet the woman of their dreams in Heaven, somehow believing that I will allow them to lie around here in bed with some beautiful gal for an eternity, but that's the last thing I want. So, I run those ads when they come in, knowing in advance that over half of them will beat a path back to the physical plane to fulfill their sexual pleasures. I want returning spirits to check in and have a cocktail with me, then get their asses back to Earth where they belong, so they can evolve in consciousness, like I intended for everyone to do in the first place. Give me another one, Son," God yelled over to Jesus, then turned to me and said, "Bottoms up, Wilde." I finished my drink.

With two glasses of champagne and a martini already under my belt, I feared that the night had only just begun, and at the rate at which I was consuming the drinks, there'd be a good chance of my waking up in the morning, cross-eyed for life. God must have somehow sensed my concern and excused himself when he told me to stay there with Jesus and catch up on old times. "Stay here, Wilde. I have to talk with someone who just walked in."

Turning to Jesus, who was behind the bar washing glasses, I was puzzled by the look on his face. I couldn't tell if it was one of peace or sadness. I wanted to break the ice but I didn't know where to begin, so I offered a compliment on the drink he made us.

"Very good martini, Jesus. What's it called?"

"A Nazarene."

"Who came up with that name?"

"Father. He comes up with all kinds of weird ideas. It never ends."

"God is rather eccentric," I said.

"Nah, you haven't seen anything yet, Buddy."

"A little too creative, is he?" I asked Jesus.

"Way too creative, if you ask me." He held up both hands with the palms facing me.

"Oh, I'm sorry, I'm so sorry." Scar tissue from Jesus's

having been hung on the cross was evident.

"That's quite all right, Buddy."

I looked away for a few moments and then thought about the role he had played in my life when I was nearly killed on my motorcycle almost twenty years prior—marking the first time I'd ever seen the "light"—I had to bring it up.

"That was you, wasn't it, Jesus?"

"At the end of the tunnel? That was me," he answered quietly.

"Wow! I get goose bumps just thinking about it. You greeted me with a sense of peace and love that was out of this world."

"Were you mad that I told you to go back?"

"Kind of," I answered Jesus. "My life up to that point wasn't anything to be proud of. I wasn't happy and didn't want to go on living that way."

"But that experience changed your life, Buddy?"

"Big time! I was hell on wheels, a fatality waiting to happen. Guess I got what I wanted though, to meet God."

"Technically, you didn't meet God. You met the Son of God. Although, it can be said that you experienced the likeness of God."

I thought back for a moment. There I was, eighteen years old, trying to find meaning in life, a purpose to it all, a reason to go on living. I even cried out one time, "If there's truly a God, let yourself be known!" And then a few days later I accidentally drove into a tree going seventy miles an hour.

"You should have been pizza," Jesus blurted out.

"What?" I asked.

"I was just reading your thoughts, Buddy, and offered that you should have been killed."

"Oh, yeah, no kidding."

"But everything leading up to that point in your life was prearranged before you incarnated, so it wasn't meant for you to die then."

"What do you mean by that?" I asked Jesus.

"Prior to leaving here on your last journey to Earth, you made all of the necessary arrangements to experience the physical plane in its entirety, and to get bogged down in the trappings of human life. The motorcycle accident was also planned right down to the smallest detail, and served as your wakeup call to catapult you into a higher state of awareness. You probably don't remember, Buddy, but your overall mission was to act as a beacon of light for other souls who would also get lost along the way—a wounded healer, of sorts," he said.

"Not according to the application Tucker showed me earlier today, before Life Review."

"Dad plays dirty sometimes," Jesus informed me.

"I should have figured as much. But you know, I did seem to help a lot of people with the way they ended up looking at life," I said.

"You were born the Week of the Teacher, Buddy— that was your main purpose for even going to Earth in the first place."

"Is that so?" I asked Jesus. "How interesting. But then, why am I here now when I could be back on Earth helping others? And if I was supposed to be this 'teacher' you speak of, why did I end up in construction?"

"I can't comment on that, and yet knowing the Almighty, you've got to believe there's a reason for it. I have to make some drinks. Need anything?"

"I'll take another one when you have time."

"Now don't overdo it, Buddy. I want you to be bright-eyed when you wake up in the morning."

"Then you'd better brush up on your healing techniques," I said, "because I came here to party."

He laughed.

"Nice talking with you, Jesus. And, hey, it's good to see you smile."

Scanning the room to see where God went, I spotted Sam Kinison, my new-found friend and favorite comedian of all time, wearing his usual trench coat and beret to corral his long hair.

"Sam!" I yelled.

He saw me sitting at the bar and came rushing over, screaming at the top of his lungs, "You made it, Wilde, ah…ahhhhhhhhhhhhhhhhhhhhhh!"

"Damn, Sam!"

"Great to see you, Buddy. It's about time. What took so long? When I talked with you earlier, I figured you'd have been here two hours ago."

"Oh…I had a little snafu with God, Sam."

"What?" he asked. "Don't tell me that, Buddy."

"Here, sit down. Let me order you another cocktail," I said, laughing at his expression. "What are you drinking, Sam?"

No one would think that for a guy who grew up in a family of evangelists like Sam did, and becoming one himself, he'd ever order a drink called a Bible Thumper. But then I thought, why not?—considering that he later left the ministry to pursue a career in comedy, which ended up leading to a life that would be laced with drugs, sex and rock'n'roll.

With the irony of that behind me, I got Jesus' attention and ordered Sam his drink. Then, my spirit guide showed up and sat next to us, asking Jesus to make him a Doubting Thomas.

"Hi, Tucker, nice suit. You clean up well," I said to him.

"Yeah, thanks, Buddy. I'll send you the dry cleaning bill for involving me in that crazy little demolition stunt of yours over in Life Review," Tucker said, smiling at me.

Then the Almighty came over and sat with us.

"What's this, Wilde," God asked, "barstool confessions?" He laughed, and then acting as if he were really drunk, leaned against the bar and yelled out to Jesus in a slur, "What's a guy gotta do to get a drink around here, bartender?"

Jesus nodded, indicating that he would make another round of drinks, and then a woman walked up to us pushing a food cart.

"Hi, Mother, let me help you with that," God said to her while putting some appetizers on a small plate.

"Take some, boys," she said to the three of us.

"What is it, Mother?" Tucker asked her.

"You've never had my Angel Wings before?" she asked. "They're really good, Tucker, and you should try some of these Drunken Shrimp. They're delicious," she said. "You dip them in this here Devil's Sauce. I made that from scratch, too."

Tucker and Sam each helped themselves to the food and then she turned to me, staring into my eyes, as if our souls had met before. God noticed the interaction between

us and then introduced me to Mother Teresa. She looked as
worn out and rundown as ever, wearing the familiar white
and blue sari, which she probably had died in.

Standing up to shake her hand, she surprised me by
putting one palm on either side of my face, and kissed my
forehead, saying, "God bless you, Buddy. What a magnifi-
cent gift you were to the world."

"Me, Buddy Wilde?" I knew that I was talking to
someone who had won a Nobel Peace Prize and wanted to
run away. "You must have me confused with someone else,
Mother. I really didn't do anything wonderful in my life, or
for mankind, like you did. I was just your average Joe Six-
pack. Sorry about the mix-up, Mother." I tried turning back
to the bar to get my drink, but she grabbed me again, this
time with both of her hands landing on my shoulders.

"No, no, no, Buddy, you don't understand," she said,
slightly shaking me and staring at me as if she were scanning every cell in my body. "God doesn't make mistakes,"
she said, "and he doesn't throw anyone away, because without the sick, the blind, the lepers, and wild animals like you,
Buddy, there would be no purpose for my life in the world—
to see the face of Jesus, behind all of the masks he wears,
and to love and serve them in the same way he would himself." She continued, "I applaud your awkward ways, Buddy
Wilde." She kissed me on the head again and then took off,
pushing her food cart, to pass out some more food.
Sam and Tucker looked at me, expressionless. God held up
his drink and made a toast. "To Buddy Wilde," he said with
a big grin, "and his awkward ways." We all laughed. It
was a hoot.

After a brief discussion among the four of us about
Mother Teresa, and how she spent all those years in the

slums of Calcutta feeding and caring for the poorest of the poor, Sam said, "Grab your drink, Buddy, and come with me. I've got some friends who want to meet you."

With that, Sam and I started through the crowd and people I didn't even know were sticking their hand out to shake mine, patting me on the back, and then I saw a familiar face.

"Is that Chief Seattle over there?" I asked, feeling a bit uneasy with this man's presence. Just one look at the deep lines in his face told volumes about his rugged life, a man who knew the full depth of both pain and sorrow, and yet a man whose veins the spirit of God ran through day and night.

"That's him, Buddy, and he hasn't moved away from that table since he came back. Just sits there looking out into space," Sam remarked.

"What's his problem?" I asked

"Ah, he's bummed out."

"About what, Sam?"

"That land deal he made. Knows he choked, and wishes he could somehow reverse it."

"Hang on a minute, Sam. Maybe I can help."

"Not now," he said, "talk with him later."

We kept walking and Sam took me over to a big round table with four or five people at it. "Everyone," he said, "I want you to meet Buddy Wilde." They each took turns standing up to introduce themselves.

"Hi, Buddy, I'm Janis Joplin. Sam's told me all about you."

"And I love your work, Janis. Only wished you could have lived longer and created more hits."

"That's the problem. I had one too many hits," she

said, half lit.

"Jimmy Hendrix, Buddy. And I had one too many hits as well. The last one killed me."

"Hey, shit happens, Jimmy," I said, "but you still get to play here, so things can't be too bad."

"Right-on, man, nothing can go wrong here," he said, playing an invisible guitar.

Just then a man pulled out a chair and sat down at the table singing *I'm a Soul Man*—da-da-da, dat-dat-da—totally oblivious to his surroundings. I asked Sam if that was who I thought it was and he affirmed that it was in fact John Belushi.

The next guy in line stood up and said, "Hi, Buddy, Stevie Ray Vaughan. I've spent many hours with Sam watching you through the Earthcam. You were very entertaining. And I have to say, Wilde, you're a man who lives up to his name." We shook hands.

"Oh, my pleasure, Stevie, you were the best. Hey, did you by any chance happen to see the tribute all your musician friends did for you a few years ago?"

"Yes, yes I did," he said, "thanks."

"It was awesome, Stevie, really was. It brought back a lot of memories," I said. "I've never seen anyone play a guitar with more passion than you."

"Well, thanks again," he said, "but that wasn't really me, Buddy. When I got up on stage, something would take over. I'd become 'one' with the instrument—like I was a conduit for some strange phenomenon that chose to run through me."

"Whatever, you're still awesome!" I praised.

"Hey, would you guys mind if I stole Sam for a few minutes?" I asked.

"No, that's cool…go ahead, we'll be right here."

I led Sam off to an empty corner in the room and then asked how he was doing and he responded, "Not bad, Buddy, not bad."

"Do you miss your life back on Earth?" I asked.

"Oh, don't start that shit," he said. "Of course I miss it—who wouldn't? I just got married the week before that drunken kid slammed into me head-on."

"I'm sorry for bringing that up, Sam. I was only hoping we could have a heart-to-heart talk. I need to tell you something," I said.

"What's that, Buddy?"

"I always wanted to meet you while you were still alive on Earth, Sam, but since that opportunity passed me by, let me just say that you touched my life with your work as a comedian in such a way that I'll be indebted to you until the end of time."

"For real?" He looked surprised.

"You have no idea, Sam."

"Huh," he said, wondering what he had done for me that was so great.

"I don't know what your experience was like with people on Earth," I said, looking directly into his eyes, "but for me, most everyone I ever ran into had a resistance to the truth, both in wanting to know it, and in speaking it."

"I'm listening," he said, not sure what this was all leading up to.

"You were different, Sam," I said. "Not only did your truth come out in the ministry, but it really showed through in your comedy. You touched a lot of lives, more than you'll ever know."

"Do you really believe that?" he asked.

I looked away and then back again. "You gave me a

license to be me, Sam—what's that say? Any time you can help a person become more of their authentic self—that to me is like the greatest gift you could ever give someone. It's like you tore down the walls of the prison I lived in and set me free."

"I've never seen myself that way," he said.

"You were much more than a comedian, Sam."

"In what respect?" he asked.

"Your message, it moved people, touched some inner part of their soul and it changed their lives!"

"No one's ever told me that before."

"Well, I am now, and you should be proud of it."

"Do you really think that I helped a lot of people with my comedy?" he asked.

"Sam, you alone, amongst all your comedic genius and crazy Jesus jokes, made it okay to be angry, okay to speak our truths, and okay to have an open relationship with God where we could say whatever was on our minds without fear of going to Hell for it."

"Whoa, stop!" He wiped a tear from his eye, then regained his composure and changed the subject.

"Where are you staying, Buddy?"

"God told me to crash here tonight, Sam."

"I was gonna say you could come over to my place after the party," he said. "I'd like to talk some more and get to know you better."

"Well, why don't you plan on hooking up with me sometime tomorrow. I wouldn't mind checking out a few of your favorite strip joints, Sam."

"Cool, we'll do that. I'll see you then, if I don't run into you before they wrap up for the evening here."

My drink was almost gone so I headed for the bar.

Along the way I noticed the Chief, still sitting there alone at the table. I pulled out a chair.

"Mind if I join you?" I asked.

"No, go ahead, sit down, young man."

"How are you doing, Chief? I'm Buddy Wilde."

"What can I do for you?" he asked.

"Well, it's not what you can do for me, Chief. It's what I can do for you. When I walked by earlier, my friend mentioned in passing that you were bummed out about some land deal you made. Is that true?"

"Yes, I'm sorry to say."

"Tell me about it, Chief."

"Long story," he said, not wanting to go into it.

"I have time," I said.

"Are you sure?" he asked.

"Yeah, lay it on me, Chief. What happened?"

"All right, then," he began. "In 1850, the President in Washington sent word that he wished to buy our land. But how can you buy or sell the sky, the land? The idea seemed strange to us. Every part of Earth was sacred to my people. We were a part of the Earth, and it was a part of us."

"Very interesting point you make there, Chief," I said, interrupting, "and you know, if a person really thinks about it, we can't actually own anything on Earth because it's all on lease to us from the universe and we have to leave it all behind when we die. Go ahead, I'm sorry for cutting in," I said.

The chief picked up where he left off.

"So I told them," he said, "that if we sold them our land, to remember that the air was precious to us, and that Earth did not belong to man, rather, man belonged to Earth."

"And what did you tell them after that?" I asked.

"Well," he said, "I stressed the fact that man did not weave the web of life, he was merely a strand in it, and whatever he does to the web, he does to himself. I was concerned with their destiny, Buddy. It was a mystery to us—what would happen when all the buffalo have been killed, what would happen when the forests were heavy with the scent of man, and the views of the hills were blotted with talking wires—the end of living, and the beginning of survival." He continued, "When the last red man has vanished with the wilderness and his memories only the shadow of a cloud moving across the prairie, would our shores and forests still be there? Would there be any spirit of my people left?"

"You had a right to be concerned, Chief," I said.

"Of course," he said, "and I told them that we loved the Earth the same way a newborn baby loves the beat of its mother's heart—and if we sold them our land, to love it as we have, to care for it as we cared for it. To hold in their mind the memory of the land as it was when they received it. To preserve the land for all children, and to love it, as God loves us all."

"Chief?" I said, feeling the need to interrupt him once again, wanting to get to the heart of the matter.

"Yes, Buddy?" he answered back, very polite.

"What were you smoking when you signed the purchase agreement?" He was flabbergasted.

"The most treasured herb of Indian ceremonies."

"That explains it. You were higher than a kite when you executed that contract."

"I don't follow."

"You were fucked up, Chief. Otherwise, you would have known better than to sell prime, sacred real estate to the white man. What did they pay you for it, may I ask?"

"I can't disclose the sale price," he said. "That was a part of the deal."

I couldn't believe what I was hearing. "Probably not much more than a song and a dance, those bastards—did the sale also include mineral rights?"

"I think so." He didn't seem to know for sure.

"Bad move, Chief, bad move. Letting go of the mineral rights is a big no-no." I shook my head.

"How was I to...?"

"I'd bet anything, Chief, that the land you love so much has since been raped and pillaged for everything it's worth! It's probably now home to a nuclear waste facility, surrounded by trailer home parks, junk yards and laundrymats."

"Returning spirits won't talk about it," he said.

"Come on," I said, "who'd want to upset the Chief? You should go take it back, call the deal off—breach of contract, your personal wishes were not honored. Verbal communications can be ruled as binding, in a court of law."

"But I wouldn't know where to begin," he said.

"Exactly! And that's where I come in. Do you know how to reincarnate, Chief?"

"I do," he said, with a bit of hesitation.

"Great, we can start there," I said. "We'll saddle up tonight and go turn that deal around."

"What right of claim would I have to it today," he asked, "my excuse for taking it back?"

"You were 'stoned,' Chief—remember? In order for anyone to execute a legally binding contract they must be of sound mind, and you were blitzed!"

"We can try," he said, with an element of doubt.

"Absolutely, as long as you are able to get us back

there in one piece," I stressed.

"I can do that," he said.

"Good, that's what I wanted to hear, Chief. Now let's go up to the bar and order you a beer. I can use another drink myself."

Standing up from the table, I pushed my chair in and was about to head for the bar when I bumped right into Tucker. He smiled. "And just where do you think you're going?" he asked.

"To the bar," I said, somehow sensing that I had just been caught trying to sneak out of Heaven.

"No, I mean with the Chief?" Tucker asked.

"Oh, that. Horseback riding!" I said with a grin.

"Buddy," Tucker said, "you can't get to Earth from here by horse. I heard everything you said and I seriously doubt that God will let it happen."

"Please," I said, "just stay out of it, Tucker."

The Chief and I walked up to the bar and Jesus, being his courteous self, asked if he could get us something to drink.

"Yeah," I said, "give me one of those Near Death Experiences, straight up, and get the Chief a beer."

"Oh, Father told you about that. Did he also mention having to bail us out of detox?" Jesus asked, with a sparkle in his eyes. The Chief didn't know what we were talking about, but I laughed, and then a Mafia-looking guy with a black trench coat pulled up the stool next to me and ordered a glass of White Lite.

"Hey, Sidekick, how've you been?"

"Not bad, J.C., and you?" he asked Jesus.

"Oh, same, same, you know," Jesus answered. "Father is still on me about my role in the Second Coming. He never quits. Hey, Buddy, have you met Sidekick? He served as your guardian angel."

"No, I haven't, actually," I said, turning to Sidekick, "but thanks for watching over me."

Sidekick laughed. "I did more than just watch over you, Buddy. I probably saved your ass about a thousand times, as well."

"A thousand times?" I asked him.

"About that," he said, "give or take a few."

"Oh, go on!" I said.

"No, really. Looking after you, Buddy, was like watching over a perpetual bolt of lightning for thirty-five years. I never knew where trouble was going to strike next."

"Was I really that bad, Sidekick?"

"Can't tell you how many times I had to save you from serious injury or death, Buddy, like the time you whacked the tree on your motorcycle. It took some real engineering genius to get that just right," he said.

"What about the time," I asked, "when I hit that gas line with the excavator and sent the whole neighborhood running for their lives?"

"Ah, now that was scary. I had to go house-to-house and blow out all the pilot lights for you," he said.

"Hey, Sidekick, did you see me take out the church roof with the wrecking ball?" I asked.

"Sure did. And I saw the priest and nun come running out with nothing on—that was a riot."

"Lucky they didn't get killed," I chuckled.

"Nah, they were being watched over by Burn and Hell, two colleagues of mine."

"Thank God for that." I turned on the barstool to

face Sidekick. "How about that time I went swimming with a friend when I was seven and almost drowned?"

"I was there," he said. "Your friend had his arm around your neck and I had mine wrapped around his, pulling you both to safety," he informed me.

"What about the time we hit black ice on the freeway and ended up in the ditch facing the wrong direction?"

"I bent the mile marker sign down so it wouldn't pierce the gas tank," he replied.

"Not far enough, though, Sidekick. It ended up taking out all the taillights."

"The snow was really deep. Did the best I could with it," he said.

"Wow, I'm impressed, Sidekick. You didn't miss a thing, did you?" I said.

"I take great pride in what I do," he said, "and I do it well."

Jesus walked over to us. "Can I get you guys anything? I'm going to take a break for a few minutes and go put on some sneakers. These sandals are killing me."

"I'm fine," I said, "but give him another beer." Jesus placed a beer in front of Sidekick and then left to change his footwear.

"Thanks, Buddy. Cheers! And welcome home," he said, tapping his glass against mine.

"Well, I don't know how to thank you, Sidekick, for saving my life, or how I'll ever repay you, but if there's anything I can ever do for you in the future, let me know."

"Don't worry about it," he said.

We talked for a few more minutes, then Sidekick got up to leave, wishing me the best for my new life in

Heaven. "Thanks again, Sidekick. I owe you one."

Jesus came back behind the bar and said, "You'll never find another angel like Sidekick, Buddy. He's one of a kind, and extremely talented," he added.

"Great guy," I said, signaling Jesus to make me another drink. "I'd highly recommend him to anyone."

"What's your poison this time, Buddy?"

"Can I get an Act of God?" I asked.

"Start drinking those and I might end up having to carry you out of here," he said.

"Here, let me give you my keys," Jesus laughed.

"I like it when you laugh," I said, paying him a compliment.

"I do that from time to time," he smiled.

"But that's not the picture the Bible paints of you, Jesus. You're totally different than what they make you out to be in there."

"Don't get me going on that subject. Here's your drink, Buddy. May the good Lord be with you," he said, placing the potent cocktail on the bar in front of me.

I picked up the drink and said to Jesus, "To whatever," and then slammed it down. "Ahhh…that was good. Give me another."

Jesus gave me the look of a wild-eyed crazy guy and said, in an impish tone, "If you say so."

I started busting up, "Oh that's too funny. Where's the men's room, Jesus?" He pointed it out for me. "Thank you," I said.

I walked over to the bathroom, admiring the fine décor along the way. Once inside I saw a long, gold-plated sink-like thing on the wall. Am I supposed to go in that, I wondered. Just then the door opened behind me. A guy walked in and stepped up, undoing his pants. He then gave me a weird look.

"Sorry, I'm new here," I said. "Didn't know if that was a urinal or a punch bowl. I almost took a sip." He laughed.

"So you're Buddy Wilde?" he asked, looking up at the ceiling with a big smile.

"The one and only," I replied.

"Hi, I'm Jim Jones," he looked over to me, "and I'd shake your hand but you can see I'm busy."

"That's okay," I said, trying to remember where I'd heard that name before.

"I was a cult leader in South America," he said.

"That's right, now I remember. You're the lunatic who made all those people drink poison and kill themselves—what, a thousand of them!"

"I wasn't thinking straight at the time," he said.

"Duh! That was really stupid of you, Jim."

"Hey, we all make mistakes."

"Yeah, but that many in a day has to be a record."

"Hey, I'm the one who has to spend the next millennium paying back the karmic debt, Buddy."

"Well, I'm glad you don't owe me anything, Jim."

"It could be worse," he said. "I've been talking with Hitler and he's a real basket case, just beside himself for killing all those innocent Jews."

"Do the math, Jim. God should make him write a million-page essay on 'When good things happen to evil people,' and you should have to proofread it."

He zipped his pants. "Maybe so."

"Don't forget to wash your hands, Jim."

I finished up in the bathroom and went back out to

the bar. Jesus had my next drink waiting for me. I sat there in silence for a moment and then asked him a question.

"Jesus," I said, "do you have any idea what God plans to do with me now that I'm back in Heaven?"

"Who knows, Buddy? I'm not even sure what he has in store for my life," he answered, just as God was coming over to join us.

"Speak of the Devil," I said, "here he is now." God began laughing, "Tucker tells me that you're going back to Earth tonight with Chief Seattle."

"That's my intention, God. He needs my help getting that land back for his people."

"Sit tight for a while, Buddy."

"But that's not fair, God—to him, or his people! They probably loved that land more than you, and I'm confident that we could go back and pull it right out from under their greedy little feet."

"Give it time, Buddy. Everything works out for the highest and best good in the long run."

"We disagree."

"Finish your drink and we'll go upstairs, Buddy. I have to get up for work in a few hours and there are a few things I'd like to talk to you about in private."

God stood up and went behind the bar, turned on the blinding overhead lights and shouted at the top of his lungs, "Drink up, you party animals, and get the hell out of here. We're closed!" With that, the whole place fell silent, and then he yelled, "Just kidding," and turned the lights back down.

"Everybody has some good.
Some hide it, some neglect it, but it is there."

Mother Teresa

Act of God

Lay the blame on Him.

Fill a tall glass with ice. Add 1 shot of Bacardi 151 Rum, 1 shot of Myers's Dark Rum, 2 oz. of orange juice and 2 oz. of pineapple juice. Mix well.

Doubting Thomas

Is there really booze in here?

In a blender combine 2 cups of vanilla ice cream, 1 shot of Chambord raspberry liqueur and 1 shot of raspberry vodka. Blend until smooth. Serve in a large margarita glass.

Drunken Shrimp

Alcoholism knows no bounds.

Place fresh, cleaned shrimp in a sauce pan. Add 3 oz. of Malibu Rum. Cover and simmer over low heat for 5 minutes, turning shrimp occasionally. Remove from stove and cool shrimp to room temperature in its own juice. Then remove shrimp from sauce pan and refrigerate. Serve with Devil's Sauce.

Devil's Sauce

It'll make you speak in tongues!

In a small bowl, add ½ cup of Heinz Tomato Ketchup, the juice from ½ of a lemon, a dash of Worchestershire sauce, 2½ tablespoons of fresh ground horseradish. Salt to taste. Allow to sit for a few hours before serving. Note: Strain horseradish by placing inside a folded paper towel to squeeze out the juice.

CHAPTER 8

A Nightcap With God

"Do you like my pad, Wilde?"

"It's not bad. I mean, it's better than any home on Earth, and certainly bigger," I said.

"A man's home should be his castle, Buddy."

We stepped off the elevator into a huge entryway with walls made of glass, floor to ceiling. The view of the city lights was breathtaking.

"This is very nice, God. You can see everything from up here, but it's no place to be in a tornado."

"Not to worry, my child, you're safe with me."

"Is that so?" I asked. "You could have had me fooled in Life Review," I said.

"What was wrong with that, Buddy?"

"Are you serious? When the room you're in starts bucking back and forth like a bull ride, and the roof caves in, followed by balls of fire—that to me is not safe. I wouldn't want to raise my daughter in an environment like that!" I said.

"I was just playing with you, Buddy. Can't a guy

have a little fun once in a while? I haven't hurt or killed anyone in my entire life," he said.

"That's not what I heard, God."

"You can't go by what others have written about me. Let's go into the living room. I'll make us a cocktail and give it to you straight from the horse's mouth. I can see that we have a lot to talk about."

God led me through the entry to an adjoining living area, where I took up a position at the bar. He went behind and started dumping booze in a blender.

"What are you making?" I asked.

"Red Sea Margaritas," he answered.

"There! That's exactly what I'm talking about, God. You parted the Red Sea to create an escape route for one group of people and then folded it in on another, killing them all."

"Never happened, Buddy."

"Are you saying that the Red Sea incident never took place?" I asked.

"I'm saying, if it did, it was not I who parted it."

"Then who did?" I asked.

"Must have been someone I created," he said.

"You're telling me that a 'man' parted the sea?"

"Who knows, Buddy? I mean, if my son can turn water into wine, heal the sick, manifest fish and loaves for five thousand, be crucified and rise from the dead three days later—then why can't a man part the sea if he wants to?"

"Because he's a man, and not the Son of God!"

"Wrong!"

"How so?" I asked.

"What did Jesus tell his disciples when they asked him about his ability to create miracles?"

"I don't remember—to get lost?"

"No, he said unto them, 'These things, and even greater things shall you do.' I gave the same power to man that I gave to Christ, but they killed the messenger before he could share the message with the masses, fearing that he would empower others with the same ability as himself."

"I wish I'd have known about that while I was still on Earth."

"You did," he said, "but there was doubt attached, just like when you prayed, and I can't bless anything that is delivered to me wrapped in uncertainty."

"I believed in the prayers I spoke, God."

"Try your drink," he said, somewhat irritated, "then I'll show you something."

I took a big gulp, "Ummm…"

"How is it?" he asked.

"Better than my prayer life," I answered.

"Put that down and come over here, Wilde!"

I set my drink on the bar and followed God over to the window.

"You see that building down there," he said. "That's Prayer Central, the clearinghouse for every little request a human being could ever make."

"Big building," I remarked. It looked to be an office building about fifty stories high and it encompassed a full city block.

"Yes, it is, Wilde. Processes over one hundred million prayer requests each day—and not a single one has ever gone unanswered."

"I'm not convinced," I said.

"It's true!" he said. "On average, ten percent of all prayers that come in each day are answered immediately, while about twenty percent are filed away to be answered in the future, and with thirty percent, I just have to say no, just wouldn't be good for them or the world at the time."

"What about all the remaining prayers, God?"

"Twenty-five percent are repeats, people who say the same prayer over and over again. One cancels out the other; they're wasting their time!"

"And to the other fifteen percent?"

"I say, 'Get a goddamned job!'"

"No shit?" I exclaimed.

"Really. A lot of people on Earth pray to me like I'm some kind of genie in a bottle that they can rub anytime they need something. I get tired of it."

"I know the feeling, God, wears a guy out." I asked him if I could sit down on the sofa. He said to make myself comfortable and that he'd be right over with the drinks. Then, sinking into the soft leather couch, I began looking around out of sheer boredom and said, "Great place you have here, God, but I'd rather be back living the only life I really know. Can't tell you how much I miss my daughter."

"You'll go back again and again," he said.

"But when—and how," I asked, "if we are actually living in the End Times?"

"Wilde, where are you coming up with all of these crazy notions? First you insinuate that I am a mass murderer; then, that I don't answer prayers; now you're telling me the End is near. What's next?"

"You don't want to know, God."

"Try me," he said, a little ticked off.

"Okay...everyone on Earth is the result of incest?"

"What?" God started laughing so hard he spilled his drink on his robe. "Who told you that?" he asked.

"Do the science, God. If you created Adam and

Eve, and then they had kids, someone had to sleep with a sibling, child or parent in order to multiply the family into the six billion hillbillies you have on Earth today."

God was still laughing. "You crack me up, Wilde. I can't believe I created such a nut. You're one crazy, absolutely fearless son of a bitch, and that's what I like about you."

"What?"

"You've got balls," he said, "just like my son. Oh, have you got balls. I can't believe it."

"Well, I'm told that I was created in your image, God. What's that tell you?"

"Hah!" He spilled again. This time he stood up and went over to the bar to wipe himself off.

"I'll take a refill as long as you're up—maybe if I drink you under the table, you'll send me back."

God was wiping the tears from his eyes, still laughing, "Fat chance, Wilde." Then he came back over with the drinks. "Here you are, Buddy. Okay, where were we?"

"You were telling me about the End Times."

"Oh, yeah…let me take a sip of my margarita first…ah, nectar of the Gods—yum!"

He began, "I know there's been a great deal of fear generated around the end of the world, and sometimes I'd like to pull the plug on that entire operation down there because, for the most part, it's all bullshit! How do they know when the world is going to end? I've got it all planned out and I can tell you that it's not going to happen anytime soon. Life on the physical plane won't cease to exist until all of its natural resources have been depleted and the last drop of drinking water tastes like raw sewage."

"Is that when the meek inherit the Earth?" I asked.

"Who'd want it then?" he asked. "I know, Buddy,

sounds totally insane, but all those messages of doom and gloom fill the offering plate on Sundays. Has more to do with economics than anything else, but tell me what you've heard. I need another good laugh. I can't believe we're having this conversation."

"Well," I said, feeling a little tipsy. "The way I was taught in Bible study about the Creation, and the End Times, is like this. First, you created Adam and Eve, put them in a beautiful garden, and told them not to eat from the Tree of Knowledge, or was that the Tree of Life, or the Apple Tree—hell, I don't remember."

"You're cut off, Wilde, if you can't remember what tree it was," God threatened.

"Give me a chance, for Christ's sake. These cocktails are starting to kick in."

"Continue," he demanded, "and stay focused."

"Okay. Then, the bitch from hell said 'Hey, Adam, look at these little puppies. I'll bet they'll make you feel like God if you hold them in your hand.' Then Adam, drunk with his growing manhood, went for it and flushed the fate of mankind right down the shitter."

God laughed, "You're getting sloshed, Wilde. Have you eaten anything today?"

"Nothing to speak of. I'm starved!"

"Got some pizza rolls I can throw in the oven."

"Is that all there is to eat around here—pizza? I had that in Life Review, no cheese!"

"Would you rather have some fish sticks, Wilde?"

"No, God—don't call Jesus. I don't want him to get out of bed. Might attract a crowd."

"Keep talking. I'll make you something to eat."

"All right, but hurry it up. I'm getting sleepy. Maybe if I just close my eyes for a few minutes…"

"Don't, Buddy, you'll get the spins," God warned.

"Let me go with you, then, God. I need to stand up and move around."

"Just sit down, and keep talking. I'll snap you out of it if you get too bad."

God walked over to the kitchen, fumbled around with some pots and pans like he was cooking up a storm, then gave me a bowl of unbuttered popcorn.

"What's this," I asked, "floor dry?"

"It'll help soak up the alcohol. Eat it, Buddy."

"Unreal!" I said. "You live in this multibillion-dollar house and you offer your guests popcorn for dinner? I can see that the acorn doesn't fall too far from the tree around here with you and Christ."

"What?" God asked.

"Are you serious? Why in the world would Jesus serve those stupid fish sandwiches when he could have popped for a seafood buffet, complete with fresh lobster and crab?"

"Ah, they were just looking for a free lunch is all."

"That figures. Anyway—like I was saying about the story behind the Creation—it doesn't make a bit of sense to me, God."

"But I still want to hear your take on it, Wilde, so tell me," he said.

I sat up on the edge of the couch to face God. "All right, according to the Bible I read, you created Adam, from who knows what, and then Eve. It said you were pissed—no wait, it said you were pleased—I get that part screwed up. Next, some shit goes down in the Garden of Eden and totally corrupts your plans for human existence. Now, one would think that you, being God, would have put a stop to the madness there. But instead, because you don't know any better, and can't see where in the hell this is all going, you wait a couple thousand years until the situation is way the fuck out of control, and then get this bright idea to send your only son down to straighten things out. He's there only a short time and comes back to Heaven looking like he spent the last three days in a knife fight, leaving behind a promise to come back to Earth and save everyone who believes in him—offering them eternal life, which to me, if you want my personal opinion, sounds like another crock of shit, but who am I to say?"

"You're Buddy Wilde. I created you—say it!"

"Just doesn't jive, God. If the word 'eternity' means 'no beginning and no end,' then how can someone step in somewhere in the middle of it all and offer us something we already have—seems a little late for that. Maybe he should have said, 'I offer you life, and offer it more abundantly.'"

"Brilliant, Wilde, absolutely brilliant! In fact…I think he did say that, now that you mention it. Want another drink to wash down the popcorn?" he asked.

"Are you trying to get me drunk, God?"

"You're already there, Buddy, and I appreciate the honesty it brings out in you. Maybe I can get your input on something else, though, a matter of utmost importance."

"Fix me another drink first, but something different. That sea salt is drying me out worse than the popcorn."

"What's your cause of death this time?" he asked.

"I don't know. You choose," I said.

"How about a Jehovah's Witness, Buddy?"

I paused for a moment, "Give me a double, one to drink and one to sleep with tonight."

"Oh, I hear you, Buddy. There's just something about them I like."

"Me too," I replied.

God went up to the bar for a minute and then came back with a whole pitcher of the cocktail, breaking my train of thought.

"You know, God," I said, "I don't want to come off as an opportunist or anything like that, but normally when I help people better understand their lives, I usually get something in return. Do you have a little token of appreciation to bless me with before the night is over?" The question caught him by surprise.

"Hmmm," he said. "Let's see, I can't offer you eternal life; you already know about that. Give me some time, Buddy, and I'll figure out what to reward you with."

"I wouldn't have asked, but I really do believe that I'm sharing with you things you would have never come up with on your own in a billion years, God."

"You're probably right, Wilde, but while I mull over what to give you, I want to hear your thoughts on another important subject, something that gnaws at me day and night: the Second Coming."

"Oh, yeah—great! That's another fine mess you got yourself into, God."

I leaned back and took a deep breath, then exhaled. "What do you want to know about it?"

"What to do?" he said.

"Well, God, I'll tell you. There's a number of options, the first one being the most practical. Tell Jesus to get back down there and straighten out that mess. You can't spend the rest of your life picking up after him, God. He needs to learn how to start cleaning up after himself."

"I agree," God said, "and I'm sure he would go if I asked, but I really don't want to put him through that again. Might cause irreparable damage. A second time around might be too traumatic, Buddy."

"Okay, then," I said, "how about sending Buddha? Have him tell everyone that Christ changed his mind, or wasn't feeling well."

"Nah, Jesus has sex appeal, Buddy. He's more Madison Avenue than Buddha. The women adored him and that's half the battle—winning them over."

I picked up my drink and finished it off, asking for a refill, trying to buy some more time to come up with yet another alternative idea for the Second Coming. God poured me a new drink.

"All right, what about this, God—have another son, Jesus II, and send him?"

"And how would I go about doing that, Wilde?"

"That's easy. Get Mary knocked up again, but this time let Joseph have a little fun with her. And that way, if things don't work out, the little bastard can't come back and blame you," I said, hoping that this was the solution God was waiting to hear.

"Not a bad idea, Wilde, but I don't think she'd go for it. She and Joseph haven't spoken in years and I couldn't expect Mary to just jump into bed with him. Women want men to seduce them from the head, down to their heart, and so on, not the other way around," he said. "Besides, Jesus is a household name, meaning everyone would have to be re-sold on a second Son of God. Won't work, Buddy."

"You're running out of options, God."

"Don't tell me that. What's left, Buddy?"

I came up with another harebrained idea, but this one was really out there. "My other thought, God, was that you could lead some scientists out to the place of Christ's death, have them find the metal stakes that held him to the cross, inspire them to extract the DNA and clone a new Christ, which would serve rather well for a Second Coming."

God jumped off the couch. "That's the craziest idea I ever heard, Wilde, but it's a good one. Only problem, though—what happens if they produce more than one Christ?"

"Perfect!" I shouted. "You could have a Third, Fourth, and Fifth Coming—make it an annual event."

God thought for a moment and said, "That might weaken the effect, Buddy. They would eventually get burned out with it. I can see it now—people would be standing around...'Oh, look, here he comes again.' Won't work."

"You're probably right, God."

"I need more ideas, Wilde," he said, pressuring me to come up with something else.

"Or, I know what you could do," I said. "Just drop the whole idea altogether, God, and be done with it. A Second Coming might not help matters anyway. People on Earth live with enough fear the way it is. They panic when the garage door opener doesn't work. What do you think is going to happen when Jesus descends from the Heavens onto the field during Super Bowl and says, 'Hi, everyone, I'm back!'?"

God scratched his head, then looked at me and said, "It'll scare the shit out of everyone!"

"And is that what you want, God, for them to change their ways? If so, save yourself the trouble. Set up a full-blown boiler room operation and have telemarketers call everyone on Earth thirty times a day until they repent!"

"Not bad, Wilde, not bad. I should try that."

"The problem you'll run into there, however, is Caller ID. They'll end up blocking your calls."

"Bastards! Should have never given away the idea for that technology. Dammit anyhow," he cussed.

"Tell you what, God. I'll give you another option, but it's the last one I have to offer."

"What, send Buddy Wilde?"

"No chance, pal." I shut that idea right down.

"I was just kidding," he said.

"No, you weren't."

God stood up to stretch his muscles to relieve some of the tension he was feeling and then said, "I hope you saved the best idea for last."

"It'll work better than any God."

"I'm curious, Wilde, tell me."

"First of all, God," I said, "if you really think about it, Jesus is only one rung on the ladder and when people think of climbing it, they do so with the idea in mind of someday reaching you."

"So, what are you saying, Wilde?"

"Send the real McCoy."

"I don't follow," he said.

"Look at it this way," I yawned. "Everything Jesus did and said on Earth was to glorify you, as you're the Big Banana God. With that said, I really think it is about time that you go down and make a presence—do a seven-continent tour, get off at every whistle stop, introduce yourself and shake hands with people. And while you're at it, perform some miracles, empty out a few hospitals, and prisons. Do a real, honest-to-goodness grass roots 'There Is a God' campaign—people eat that shit up!"

"Now that's the best idea you've had so far, Buddy. What's the downside?"

"They'll have your ass nailed to a tree within seventy-two hours—guaranteed!"

"Do you really think so?" he asked.

"Listen to me, God, anyone who tries to change the world either ends up on a cross or gets shot. One way or another, we kill 'em!"

"That's true, isn't it? God, how I wish I could just retire and turn everything over to my son," he said. "I'm so tired of always having my mind preoccupied with all this crap."

"Then why don't you?" I asked.

God sat back and thought for a moment, looking up with his head against the couch and his eyes closed, and then said, "I'd like to, but Jesus won't go along with it. I offered him the throne once before, but he turned it down flat."

"How come?" I asked.

"Because he's a spoiled brat! Why should he take on all the responsibility that comes with being the Almighty when he can live with me rent-free forever and have anything he wants?"

"That's not..."

"It's a fact! I'll prove it. Where in the hell's my phone—watch, this always gets him." (Bleep-bleep) "Jesus Christ, Son, what are you doing to that poor woman down there? I can hear you eighty floors up—give it a break!" (No response) (Bleep-bleep) "Rise and shine, Savior, Daddy-O has to talk with you."

(Bleep-bleep) Jesus answered. "I was sleeping, Father. What can I help you with?"

(Bleep-bleep) "The Wild One and I were just having a little nightcap. Called to see if you wanted to join us for one?"

(Bleep-bleep) "It's two in the morning."

(Bleep-bleep) "Actually, Son, I'm calling to tell you that I've decided to retire and if you don't take the throne, I'm going to name Buddy…"

(Bleep-bleep) Jesus cut in, "I really don't want it, Dad, and if you appoint the Wild One, that's fine by me."

God set the phone down and picked up his drink.

"You see, I told you he won't have any part of it. Looks as if your new name is 'God,' Wilde."

"*Me!* What in the hell would I want to be God for? You've gotta be out of your mind!" I shouted.

"Why not?" he asked.

"Yeah, right, and put up with all the bullshit that you have to contend with each day? No thanks!"

"I'm serious, Wilde!"

"So am I! Your own son doesn't even want anything to do with it. Hellooo."

"Want me to make you a new drink?" he asked.

"Not if this shit keeps up. In fact, I'd much rather you just send me back to Earth and pretend we never met."

God walked over to the bar. "What shall we have this time, Wilde? How about a Messiah?"

"Like another drink is gonna help matters. Why would you want to make me God, anyway?"

"Because I'm tired, Buddy. I've been the kingpin for quite some time now, longer than you may think. It's time for me to move on."

"And what would you do with this new-found freedom, God, hypothetically?"

"Well, for one, I might sober up. That's why I drink all the time. It helps take my mind off of things. That's how I escape the never-ending pressures of being the Almighty."

"Then what would you do?"

"Probably travel. I want to see what's out there, Buddy. Maybe even visit some of these other planets I created and see what those people are up to nowadays."

"Are you telling me that there are other forms of life as in civilizations, somewhere in the universe?" I asked. God told me that everything happened so fast and so long ago that he really couldn't remember all that he created. "And you'd trust me to hold down the fort all on my own while you were out gallivanting around the universe?"

"Absolutely! Without question," he said.

"Okay, tell me this. If I agreed to take the position— which I'm not, just being inquisitive—how long would I have to be God, and what's it pay?"

"Hell, I don't care," he said. "Pick your own terms, Buddy. Work as little as you want, and you could never write yourself a paycheck big enough to overdraw my account. I'd leave that all up to you, because you'd be God."

Wow! I had to stop and think. After all, how often does an opportunity to be God come around? But then, if being God is so great, why is he willing to give up the position, I wondered.

"I don't know," I said. "Something's not right here. You wouldn't by any chance be looking for a fall guy, someone to take the hit when the planet goes to pot and six billion screaming idiots come back looking for the asshole that created this whole mess, would you?"

"Interesting point, Wilde, I never thought about that. And it might not be a bad idea to be to hell and gone when that day comes."

God walked away and then returned, handing me a glass of champagne, and offered a toast, "To Buddy Wilde, the next Almighty!"

"Not so fast," I yelled. "I'll have to sleep on it and I

can't promise you anything, God."

"That's right. It is getting late, Wilde. Maybe we should go to bed and talk about it tomorrow. I have to get up for work in twenty minutes."

"Are you serious?"

"Got to answer some prayers, Buddy."

"After drinking all night?"

"That's right."

"I don't know if I like the sound of that."

"Take my bed," God instructed. "There's a clean robe in the closet. I'll have room service press your tux and have it ready for when you get up."

"Are you going to sleep in, God?"

"Probably not. Jesus usually comes by in the morning and cooks breakfast. I'll wake you when it's time to eat."

*"Three highballs, and I think I'm
St. Francis of Assisi."*

Dorothy Parker, *Just a Little One*

Red Sea Margarita

It'll swallow you up.

In a blender, combine 2 oz. of Jose Cuervo tequila, 1 oz. of Triple Sec orange liqueur, and 4 oz. of frozen or canned red cherries in juice. Mix until smooth. Add 1½ cups of shaved ice and blend until slushy. Serve in a margarita glass, rimmed with lime and sea salt. Garnish with a wedge of lime.

Jehovah's Witness

It will keep coming back to haunt you.

Fill a shaker glass with ice. Add 1½ shots of vodka, 1½ shots of peach schnapps and 1 shot of Sambuca liqueur. Strain into shot glasses. Makes 2 shots.

CHAPTER 9

Breakfast With Christ

"Buddy, Buddy, get up."

"Hah? What?" I grumbled.

"Come on, Buddy, get up. Breakfast is ready," he said, wiggling the bed.

"Oh...my head, it's killing me. I think my aneurysm ruptured again," I complained.

"Nah, can't be, just a little hangover is all."

"What time is it, anyway?" I asked.

"Time to eat. Shake it off and come out to the kitchen while the food is still hot."

"Like this?" I asked, rubbing my eyes.

"Yes, and hurry on. I don't have all day," God said, helping me out of bed.

"Slow down, give me a minute...how long did I sleep for, anyway, God?" He responded that it didn't matter.

With God at my side and one arm over his shoulder, I walked out to the kitchen wearing a white robe trimmed in gold, with God half holding me up. Jesus was putting a bowl of fresh fruit on the table.

"Look, Son, here's the next, new-and-improved Almighty," he said, making fun of me. Jesus glanced over and laughed, "Welcome to the throne, Buddy. It'll be a pleasure working with you, I'm sure,"

"I said I would 'think about it,' God. Where would you like me to sit?"

"At the head of the table, of course," God said.

In front of me was a tall glass of tomato juice. It looked to be just what the doctor ordered. I picked it up and swallowed all of it in one drink, which was a big mistake.

"Holy Christ! What is this?" I shouted, looking for something else on the table to put out the flames. I'd never tasted anything so spicy hot in my entire life.

God started laughing, while Jesus handed me a glass of water, saying, "Dad calls it a Screaming Bloody Mary."

"My lord! It tastes more like a drink from the Lake of Fire!" I said, wanting to die.

"Best known cure in the universe for a hangover. Has fresh jalapenos in it," God said.

"Yeah…and I'll bet you start each day with one of these," I said.

"Sit down," he said to Jesus. "I'll lead us in prayer." God put his hands together and began. "Our Father, who…"

"Stop! Stop! Stop!" I screamed. "I'm so…if I have to say that one more time, I'm gonna puke my guts out! Can't someone think up another prayer? That's the only thing they know to say on Earth."

"Ah, the heck with it then," God said. "Let's eat."

"Thanks," I said, "and thank you, Jesus. Everything looks wonderful, some good food."

God was the first one to finish eating, since his entire breakfast consisted of a Bloody Mary and a piece of toast. He stood up wiping his mouth and then excused himself from the table.

"I have to run some errands," he said. "Why don't you two hang out until I get back? Here's the morning paper if you get bored."

Sitting there with Jesus, a very quiet type of man, I picked up the *Good News Tribune* and opened it to the Classifieds.

"No shortage of work in Heaven, is there, Jesus?" I said, trying to make conversation.

"Are you looking for a job, Buddy?"

"Just checking things out. God asked me last night to take over the throne so he can retire, but I don't think I want it." Then I spotted something in the Employment section that caught my attention:

Shipping Clerk Wanted!
Bright individual with good communication skills needed to assist with helping spirits return to Earth. Must be a self-starter, detail-oriented, and work well with others. Hours and salary negotiable. For more information, contact Diego at 555-SHIP.

After reading the ad, the idea came to me that if things didn't work out for me in the afterlife, I could always get a job in Shipping and then one day, when no one was looking, I could send myself back to Earth. I said to myself, "In fact, why not get the job now and reincarnate back into my old body so I can see my daughter once again. People who've been declared dead wake up in the morgue on occasion. That's a great idea."

"Jesus, is there a phone around here I can use? Need to call about a job," I said.

"In the other room," he answered.

"Call straight out?" I asked.

"No, first dial 9, then the number," he said. "Did you happen to see the Comics section, Buddy?"

"It's in there somewhere," I said. "You'll have to look." I couldn't punch the keys fast enough. The phone rang and rang, and then someone answered.

"Shipping. Diego speaking."

"Oh, hi, Diego. This is Buddy Wilde calling about the position for shipping clerk. Is it still available?" I had my fingers crossed.

"Funny you should call, this is the first inquiry I've had since placing the ad over two weeks ago," he said.

"Well, I never worked in a warehouse before, Diego, and I'm not sure what it is that you actually do there, but if you would be so kind as to take me under your wing, I'm certain I'd catch right on—for some reason this job intrigues me."

Diego sounded relieved to think that someone was actually interested in filling the position and then asked me if I could come in today and fill out an application.

"I'm not sure," I said. "I'm new in town and haven't had any chance to learn my way around yet, but maybe I can get someone to bring me over."

He paused for a moment and then asked if I would be going to Happy Hour later in the afternoon.

"I don't know, Diego, let me ask."

I yelled out, "Jesus, do you know anything about Happy Hour tonight, and if I'll be going?" He responded, "With my father around, you can almost count on it, Buddy. I've never known him not to go."

I got back on the line, "Guess I'll be there, Diego. How about we talk more then?"

"That'll work, Buddy. I look forward to meeting you.

I hung up the phone and went back into the kitchen. Jesus was still sitting at the table reading the comics. "What did you find out, Buddy?"

"It's still available and from what I can tell, it sounds as if the boss wants to hire me. I have an interview with him tonight at Happy Hour."

"Well, I hope you get the job, Buddy, providing Father doesn't talk you into taking the throne between now and then."

"Thanks, Jesus…and you know, I want to do the right thing, but I'm not sure what that is," I said.

"Well, if you're at all concerned with doing the will of God, don't be," Jesus said. "Ever since I came back here from the cross, he hasn't had any will other than to party. In reality, the Almighty doesn't give a hoot about anything— he's very Zen-like. To him," Jesus continued, "there is no right or wrong in the world, no good or bad, no evil or holy, no overpowering will or things-to-do-list—everything just *is,* the way it is."

"Are you saying he doesn't care about the Universe, or the people in it?" I asked.

"No, what I'm saying is that he loves us all dearly. And in that love he finds the strength to let the world and everything in it be what it wants to be and do what it wants to do. He's not a control freak like a lot of people would have you believe."

"But how can he be so carefree? That'd be like him saying that everything is just the way it should be."

"It is, Buddy, and if the Almighty tried to right all the wrongs in the world, there wouldn't be a world! What people don't realize is that everyone on Earth is causing harm to another, and/or the planet, at some level," he said. I was still puzzled.

"How do you figure that there wouldn't be a world if he corrected everything that's wrong with it?" I asked.

"Let me get another cup of coffee. Want some?" Jesus asked.

"Yes, please, hold the vodka. I'm joking."

Jesus poured our coffee and sat down. "Okay, where'd we leave off?" he asked.

"You were telling me what would happen if God righted all the wrongs in the world."

"How can I best explain this to you, Buddy—ah, got it! Now pay attention and try to follow along, Buddy. I'm going deep, and considering that you were up drinking all night with the Almighty, this will fit right in."

"Go ahead, I'm listening," I said.

"All right." He began with a statement followed by a question, "Every year thousands of people are killed in alcohol-related automobile accidents. So tell me, what would be the most surefire way for God to eliminate that problem, or to right the wrong in this scenario?"

"Dry up all the booze on Earth and kill anyone who tried to make more," I said.

"Okay, and what would happen if he did that?"

"A lot of stuff," I said. "I once read that there's over four thousand different jobs related to making a No. 2 pencil. Seems that everything in the world is somehow interconnected."

"That's true," Jesus replied, "but give me some examples. What effect would it have on the world?"

"Well, I don't know for sure, but being a businessman, I'd have to say that it would have a huge impact on the economy."

"Who would it affect, Buddy, with no more booze or drunk drivers in the world?"

"Well, the first ones that come to mind for me are the liquor manufacturers, breweries and wineries, their workers—truck drivers, office, warehouse and sales people, accountants, and the banks and leasing companies that finance everything. It would probably hit the advertising industry pretty hard, not to mention all the various media and the news rooms that cover the stories."

"You ate out once or twice a day, Buddy. What about bars and restaurants?"

"That's big! People would stay home and cook if they couldn't go out and have a cocktail with dinner. A lot of waiters and waitresses and bartenders would be looking for work, most food establishments that served alcohol would go under, you probably couldn't get a job washing dishes, and I can't tell you how many cab drivers would have to pull over and park their cars permanently."

"Would it hurt the stock market, Buddy?"

"Without a doubt! Brokers, underwriters…"

"What about the medical profession?" he asked.

"Unbelievable! Doctors and nurses would be laid off, not to mention paramedics and tow truck drivers and accident scene investigators. Pharmaceutical companies and medical equipment makers would also feel it."

"Who else?" Jesus asked.

"Let me see…funeral home directors, flower shops, greeting card artists, casket makers, automobile manufacturers, body shops, insurance companies, policemen, judges, clerks of court, a whole gob of attorneys, process servers, treatment centers, and prison personnel. It's endless!"

"Buddy, you haven't even scratched the surface yet, much less factored in the ripple effect."

"I know, but what's your point? Are you telling me it's okay to get all liquored up and then go out and plow into a car full of innocent people?"

"No, what I'm saying is that no matter what people do in life, nothing ever goes wrong in the eyes of God. To him, everything is in perfect order," he said. "There's a divine reason for everything that happens in the universe."

"But we have to punish bad people, or else..."

"Don't be too quick to judge another, Buddy. Leave that to those who live in fear. The world is full of them. If you do it, you are also judging the one who created those being accused, in essence saying to the Almighty, 'We do not approve of this person you created, or the way in which you made the world to be.' And then, if God actually wanted to punish humans for their every little error, he would make everyone live to be 150, regardless of their health."

"But you still haven't answered my question!"

"Just see the love of God in everyone you meet, Buddy, and the divine perfection in everything that happens, even when the worst comes before you."

"That's easy for you to say, Jesus. You're the Son of God, up here playing it safe. But where I come from, it's wicked!"

"Well, I didn't want to go into this, but it looks like I'll have to. Years ago God wrote the Law of Karma, or cause and effect, creating an accounting system that keeps track of every action that ever takes place in the universe. It's infallible, and a long story to tell someone how it all works. With that, I'll just say that you don't have a thing to worry about, Buddy. Every loveless act in the world gets balanced out when the time is right."

"Everything, including every little sin?" I asked.

"Yes, everything," he said. "However, I should also mention that the word 'sin' comes from an old archery term. It means 'to miss the bull's eye,' which is 'love.' So in reality," he said, "you need not even concern yourself with thoughts of sin or 'who sinned,' because the Law of Karma will take care of everything in due time. With that," Jesus added, "what human beings need to do is become conscious of the love, or lack thereof, behind every thought, action, and reaction that they themselves create."

I couldn't take it anymore and unconsciously stood up using the Lord's name in vain. "Jesus Christ! Oh...I'm sorry, Lord. I'm so sorry for saying that." I sat back down.

"Better to use my name in vain than not at all. I can work with that; it tells me I have some sort of significance in your life, some level of relationship. That's better than being a complete stranger," he said, trying to comfort me.

"I know, Jesus, but please excuse my expression. I'm just so blown away with the things you are sharing with me. You've got to be the coolest guy I've ever met. How do you do it?"

"Practice," he answered.

"And what do you practice, 'forgiving and forgetting,' or something like that?" I asked.

"Kind of," he said. "But you have to understand that 'forgetting' is 'for-getting,' or in other words, to 'get' something in life; whereas, 'forgiving' is 'for-giving,' or to 'give' something to life."

"And was that your sole reason for going to Earth, to teach us that?" I asked.

"Actually, my purpose was bigger than that, Buddy. I went down there to offer forgiveness, teach unconditional love, and to demonstrate that there is life after death."

"Unfrickinbelievable!" I exclaimed.

"In a nutshell, that's it, Buddy. Would you like some more coffee?" he asked.

"No thanks, Jesus. What I should do is lie down for a while and let this all soak in."

"Any more questions?" he asked.

"Maybe. Hang on for a minute," I told Jesus.

Sitting across the table from this incredible Man of God, I was in complete awe. Trying to describe him with our present vocabulary would be more fruitless than when I tried explaining my near-death experience to others. I was at a total loss for any form of intelligence.

"Tell me, Jesus," I said, "and I've been meaning to ask you this since I came back to Heaven—who cleaned all those fish, and baked all that bread?"

"Who squeezed all those grapes when I was making wine?" he answered.

"Ah, there you go again, answering a question with a question. You were famous for that."

"Anything else, Buddy?"

"Yeah, a few more. Tell me something else, providing it's not a trade secret. How'd you heal that leper?" I asked, trying to keep my voice down.

"What leper?" he asked.

"Are you kidding? Don't tell me they also made that up when they wrote that damned Bible."

"I didn't see any leper. All I saw was a man that had detached himself from the grace of God. Then, seeing that love in him is what produced the cure."

"Well, that's pretty incredible, Jesus. Maybe you should go back down and teach that to the medical profession, to see beyond the mechanics of disease. The health care industry needs your help. It's overwhelmed."

Jesus laughed. "And go sit in jail? No thanks. The AMA would have a panic attack and lock me up for practicing medicine without a license!"

"Then go back as a research scientist, or a child prodigy, and create some 'wonder drugs'—anything. They need your help badly."

"I'd like to teach a course using hands-on healing techniques, but I don't think I'll be going back."

"But you should go back. You have to go back, if for nothing else, then at least to rewrite that obnoxious book of yours. I've never seen such a disaster!"

"I know," he said, admitting that it's all screwed up, "but that's how the media works sometimes, Buddy— twisting, turning, and distorting things to serve their own needs and desires. Anything else, Buddy? I have to use the bathroom. Coffee runs right through me."

"Give me a second."

I thought for a moment, then it came to me.

"Just one more question. I have to know, did you actually walk on water?"

"Nothing to it, piece of cake," he said.

"It's not hard to do?" I asked, doubting in my ability to actually defy the laws of physics.

"There is no degree of difficulty in creating miracles, Buddy. A big one is no tougher than a small one. If we have time later, I'll show you how."

"Would you? That is so awesome! Thank you, and thanks for having breakfast with me. I really enjoyed talking with you, but I'm still confused."

"About what?" he asked.

"Who's more radical, Jesus—you or Sam?"

"Sam is," he laughed. "I have to pee." He got up and walked toward the bathroom.

"I'm not convinced. Looks like a tossup. I'm gonna lay down for a while, do you mind?"

"Be my guest," he said.

"Do you need any help with the dishes or putting things away?" I asked.

"I'll call the maid," he responded.

"Must be nice being the Son of God," I said.

"It has its advantages."

I got up and walked over to the window to check out the daytime view of the city. Jesus didn't shut the door all the way, so I could hear him in there.

"You can see everything from up here," I said in a loud voice.

Jesus yelled back, "That's the idea. God can look down on everyone, but they can't see him."

"Don't tell me, is that a Harley-Davidson dealership right below us?"

"Sure is. Dad has a huge collection of bikes and he usually goes riding on the weekends."

I scanned the buildings below looking for other familiar signs of life as it was on Earth.

"What goes on in that big complex on the hillside?"

Jesus came out drying his hands with a towel. "Oh, that," he said. "They're responsible for keeping track of all the hairs on your head, Buddy."

"Really? What a waste," I said, "like it really matters how many hairs I grow or lose each day."

"It does to God," Jesus said.

"Yeah, but that's taking things a little too far."

"Then, He took the cup, gave it to His disciples and said..."

Luke 22:17

Screaming Bloody Mary

A drink from the Lake of Fire.

In a blender, combine 2 oz. of peppered vodka,
½ fresh jalapeno pepper and ¼ clove of fresh
garlic. Blend on high speed to mince. Then
add 2 oz. of vegetable juice, 2 oz. of tomato
juice, a few shakes of celery salt, juice from a
lemon wedge, ½ tsp. of Worchestershire sauce,
¼ tsp. of Tabasco and blend on low speed only
to mix. Add salt and pepper to taste. Pour
into tall glass of ice. Garnish with a stick of
celery.

Walk on Water

It can be done.

Fill an old-fashioned glass with ice. Add a
shot of Johnny Walker Red Scotch. Fill with
unsweetened lemon-flavored seltzer water.
Garnish with a lemon twist.

CHAPTER 10

Wake Up! It's Happy Hour

"Buddy, wake up, it's Happy Hour," God said, shaking me as if the place were on fire.

"Let me sleep."

"No, come on. They have 2-for-1 drink specials until seven. Let's go!"

"Do I have to?"

"Yes, now move it. Your tux is not back yet, so you'll have to wear a robe."

"Oh, wonderful! Let me take a shower first."

"Only if you hurry," God said. "Jesus is waiting."

Dreading the fact that I had to get up to go on what might end up being another long drinking bout with God, I walked over to the bathroom, still half asleep, and turned on the faucet. Rusty water dribbled out.

"What the hell? Who forgot to pay the water bill?" I screamed, but no one heard me. "Great! My hair looks like hammered shit. This is going to be fun…" Then I remembered that I had to meet up with Diego to talk about the Shipping Clerk position.

I put on a clean white robe, trimmed in gold, and walked into the living area picking the crud out of my eyes. God and Jesus were waiting in the hall.

"Have either of you guys tried using that shower within the past hundred years?" I asked.

They looked at each other like it worked fine for them. It never dawned on me that they could probably just think themselves clean and it would be so.

"Come on, Buddy, the elevator is waiting." As the doors closed behind us, Jesus whispered to me to hang on.

"Show Buddy zero gravity, Son."

Jesus pushed the button and we all hit the roof, plunging downward like a falling rock. At about the tenth floor, we landed softly on our feet again.

"I really didn't need to experience that right now, God. I'm still hung over from last night."

"Hey, Buddy," he said, "we could have taken the stairs. They're really a bitch!"

The elevator door opened on the first floor and God's hotrod of a golf cart was there and running.

"Hop in up front with Boy Wonder," God told me. "Show him how the nitro works, Son."

"Okay," Jesus replied. "Hold on to your robes!" We zoomed off.

"Try to bury the speedometer, Son!"

I yelled over to Jesus, "Didn't we just pass that place we were at last night?"

"About a quarter mile ago," he said.

"Then where are you taking me?" I asked.

"There, but Dad said to bury the speedo." Jesus had

the pedal to the floor.

"Ah, shit! Slow her down, Son. I don't think the house is big enough. I'll have to add on. Turn around and take us back to the Bang," God said.

"The 'Bang'? What's that, God?"

"The Big Bang Bar & Grill," he answered.

"Oh, yes, of course," I said.

As seemed customary, Jesus opened the door and gestured for me to follow, with God right behind me. Two hundred people stood up and gasped! God walked over to my side and lifted my hand up in the air with his.

"Ladies and gentlemen, please allow me to introduce the new Almighty, Buddy Wilde!"

The crowd stood there dumbfounded. I pulled away from God.

"What? No way, pal. We have to talk—now!" God knew I was pissed.

"Buddy? We already discussed this last night," he said.

"But I never said I'd do it!" I said, backing up even farther from God.

"Come on, Bud, what's the matter?"

"Don't 'Bud' me, dammit. You know full well what's the matter—you set me up!" I screamed. God began scanning my body from head to toe, as if he were going to rip me to shreds. Everyone present remained dead silent.

After what seemed like an eternity, God looked out over the crowd and spoke: "I've never created anyone more crazy or hard to please than Buddy Wilde, folks. He doesn't want to stay here, he doesn't want to take my son's place in returning to Earth as the Second Coming of Christ, and he doesn't even want to take the throne and be God. Do any of you know what he wants?" he summoned the crowd, but there where no takers.

Then a voice shouted from across the room, "Ask him!" It was Jesus, speaking from behind the bar.

"All right, then," God hollered, "I will. Tell me what you want to do, Buddy, and be specific."

I was so mad that I didn't know whether to cry or kill someone. I responded, "The only thing I want to do is go back home and see my daughter again."

God paused, then asked, "Are you serious, Buddy?"

"You obviously don't know how serious I am, God. I was gonna ride out of here with Chief Seattle, until Tucker went and blew the whistle on me. And then, if you really want to know, I was supposed to meet someone here to-night from Shipping for a job interview. I was gonna send my ass right back to where it came from!"

"Are you so desperate," God asked, "that you would actually give up the chance to take the throne and become the Almighty?"

"Again, you don't know. You don't even know me, God, or my heart."

"Any chance you might reconsider?" he asked.

I walked over to the bar, hoping Jesus might offer to make me a drink. Every eye in the room was locked in on me, awaiting my response.

"If you, God, don't allow me to go back and at least say goodbye to my daughter—maybe even take her to Disney World, like I promised her just a few days ago—perhaps make a few amends, then you might just as well turn me back into dust, and that's my final plea!" I sobbed.

"You'd rather do that than become the Almighty?"

he asked. "Am I hearing you correctly?"

"Yes, you are," I answered.

God threw both hands in the air, walked over toward me, jumped up on top of the bar and yelled, "Cut! That's a wrap. Great performances, everyone. Tucker, you win Best Actor on this one. The drinks are on me."

"What?" I was taken aback. "What's this, another one of your sick fucking jokes?" I asked God.

"No," he answered, "I'm sending you back to your life on Earth, Buddy, and you're leaving tonight!" Everyone cheered.

I stood there speechless, then just managed to get a couple of words out: "I am?" The crowd laughed.

God came down off of the bar in front of me and said, "That you are, Buddy." He ordered Jesus to make everyone a Nazarene, and then he turned to me, saying, "I have to level with you, Buddy. You don't really even belong here. It's not your time yet, but I'm glad you could drop in and visit. I can't tell you the last time I had this much fun." He was smiling.

I was puzzled, "Why did you call me back, then?"

"I didn't," he said. "You came in on your own."

"No way," I said.

"Yes, way," he replied. "That ruptured aneurysm you suffered that caused your journey here? Those are caused by a copper deficiency. What happens is that the elastic fibers start breaking down, and then—wham!—there you are, knock-knock-knocking on Heaven's door."

I was shocked. "Well, how was I to know?"

"Buddy," he said, "the first signs for early detection are white, gray and silver hair. Have you looked in a mirror lately?"

"I did before we came down here tonight."

"Too late," he replied.

"So I really do get to go back?" I asked.

"No, you don't get to go back," he said. "You *have* to go back. Staying here is not an option—your life isn't over yet." Then he told me to say goodbye to everyone and get the hell out of there before he changed the rules.

With a million thoughts running through my mind, and sensing I had very little time to sort everything out, I sat down on a barstool and said to God, "Let me have another drink first."

He looked at me and then at Jesus and said, "One more, Son, then he's cut off!"

Jesus showed his excitement for my getting to leave by joking with the Almighty, "Would you mind if I mixed up one of my Near Death Experiences for Buddy before he goes?"

"Yes, I would mind!" God yelled. "And the next time you get thrown in the puker with your twelve loser friends that won't get a job, don't call me." Jesus laughed and then handed me a martini.

"That sounds like something Sam would say," I remarked, taking a drink. "And speaking of the disciples, where are they? I haven't seen them yet."

God pointed to a long table with a dozen guys sitting next to each other on the back side, as if they were all sewn together. "Have you ever seen such a sorry-looking bunch, Wilde?" he asked.

"What are they doing," I asked, "a reenactment of the Last Supper?"

God laughed, shaking his head. "How anyone can hang out with those guys is beyond me. I get nauseous just looking at them," God said.

"Hey, that reminds me," I said, "where's Sam? I have to see him before I go, and I can't leave without saying goodbye to Chief Seattle."

God gave me a look, saying with his eyes that it was time for me to leave.

"What, God? I was serious about trying to help him get his land back. Just let me talk to him and then I'll go, I promise you."

"Well, don't screw around," he said. "Every cell in your body is probably wondering where in the hell you are right now, Buddy. It's going to turn cold, stiff and blue if you don't hurry."

Then I asked God how many years I would have left in my life back on Earth and he said, "I can't answer that, Buddy. However, I'll tell you this: Live your life moment by moment—not in the future or the past. It goes a lot farther that way," he added.

Just then Chief Seattle walked up and ordered a pitcher of beer. He turned to me, putting one hand on my shoulder. "Buddy," he said, "I want to say 'thanks' for listening to me yesterday, and I appreciate your concern. Granted, I wouldn't mind getting that land back for my people, but I think the statute of limitations for making a claim has probably run out by now."

"But there must be something I can do, Chief."

"There is," he said. "Go back and hold everything sacred, including the land you walk upon."

"I'll do that, Chief, you can count on it," I said.

Sam came up to the bar with Catchme and Doome. "Damn, Buddy, I wish you could have hung around a little longer. I wanted to take you out on the town and show you some of the sights."

I laughed and said, "Damn, Sam, I see two right behind you." He smiled, and then filled the whole room with his scream, "Ah...Ahhhhhhhhhhhhhhhhhhhhhhhhhhhhhh!"

What a gem, I thought to myself, and then said, "I'm really going to miss you, Sam."

"You'll be okay, Buddy," he said. "But if worse comes to worse, just pop in one of my videos and I'll be there with you, watching through the Earthcam." He gave me a hug and turned to leave.

"Wait, Sam! I wanted to ask, will you be coming back to the physical plane anytime soon?"

"No, not for a while, Buddy," he said. "I'm going to hang out here and wait for my family and friends to return. But you can tell them all a big 'Hello' from me in the meantime."

"I'll try to look them up when I get back," I said.

Then he started walking away with the two women. They both turned to me, smiling, and said, "Good luck, Buddy."

"Yeah. Thanks, girls," I said, thinking to myself, "maybe next time, huh?"

"All right, Buddy, drink up. It's time to go," God said, trying to hurry me.

"Goodbye, Jesus," I said, leaning over the bar to give him a hug. "I'll miss you, and if you ever decide to come back to Earth, look me up. The same goes for you, God. I'm in the book!"

Jesus said, "Okay, Buddy, and tell everyone on Earth that I say 'Hi.'"

"Well then, let's go," I said to God, totally excited.

"I'm as ready as I'll ever be."

"Not so fast," he said. "You're not getting out of here that easily—I want you to do something for me."

"And what would that be?" I asked.

"Promise me that when you get back to Earth, you'll tell everyone about your experience here in Heaven, and that they're all invited to join me for cocktails, and what a great host I am."

I wasn't sure just how the Almighty intended for me to do that, exactly, so I asked, "What are you saying, God, go door-to-door and witness?"

"No, stupid, write a book about it, and sell a billion copies. Use your head, Wilde!"

"But I'm not a writer, God, and I don't know the first thing about promotion or sales."

"Then learn! And if all else fails, there's a guy—I want to say in Florida—with 1001 marketing ideas. Look him up on the Internet."

"If you say so, but don't blame me if this whole idea blows up in your face. And by the way, what do you plan to get out of all this?"

"Exposure. I'll do anything for a story about me."

"And what if it doesn't fly, or worse, what if I turn it around and use this experience against you?"

"I don't care what you do, Wilde. Just get it out there. I'd much rather have you say something negative or even bad about me than to say nothing at all."

"All right, but at least get me started. What should I call it?" I asked.

"I don't know," he said. "Be creative, use your imagination. You'll think of something. Here's my number to call if you get hung up, but don't give it out to anyone—and I mean *no* one."

"I can actually call you from Earth?" I asked.

"Certainly. I invented wireless. Now drink up, because you're not leaving here with my glass."

"Wait! One more question, God. How do I explain my absence for the last two days?"

"You won't have to, Buddy. Your entire life is but the 'blink of an eye' to me."

"That's it?" I started thinking about what a rip-off that was. "You should redo that, God, make it 'two blinks' or a 'yawn'—there's just not enough time to get our life right, much less enjoy it."

"That's what reincarnation is for, Buddy. You can go back as many times as you like, and master the physical plane at your own pace," he said.

"Are you for real? I mean, no joke?"

"Absolutely! Would you ever take your precious little six-year-old daughter to a theme park, spend two hours walking around looking at all the fun things to do, then turn to her and say, 'Pick one ride, sweetheart, and then we have to leave'?"

"Are you kidding me? She'd throw a fit!" I answered.

"And likewise, people come back here kicking and screaming all of the time, because they believe they'll never get to go back were the action is."

"I just couldn't do that to her, God."

"Exactly, Wilde! So then, why would I ever go through all the trouble to create a humongous, naturally beautiful theme park—with rivers, lakes, streams, oceans, beaches, forests, mountains, stars, a sun and moon—where there's literally billions of things to do—then turn to you and say, 'You only get one shot at this,

Buddy, make it good!' No, I wouldn't do that, either. I'm
not that pressed for time! And if you really think about it,
why would I want all you yahoos hanging around here anyway? I go through enough booze as it is!"

"That you do, God, and I'm concerned. Are you
going to be all right—you know, with the bottle?"

"Buddy, let me tell you something. I have never
been intoxicated a day in my life—but it's a hell of a lot of
fun to act like it!" He continued, "I could drink all the wine
and beer and hard liquor in the universe in one sitting and it
wouldn't phase me. I transcend it all. Nothing can touch
me. I'm just naturally drunk with bliss," he said.

"So then what are you telling me, God, that this is
all some kind of an act, or an illusion?" I asked.

"Well, I did go a little out of my way to put on a
show for you," he said smiling. "But in reality, this is your
reality, and your life on Earth is an illusion. There's absolutely nothing real about it, Wilde. Just look at anything
that appears to be made of physical matter under a high-
powered microscope and you'll see there's nothing there
but these tiny wiggles of energy surrounded by vast amounts
of black empty space. At its very core, the entire universe
and everything in it is made up of nothing more than pure
energy. And if I'm not mistaken," God said, "I believe there
are some scientists back on Earth who figured out that this
energy is eternal and nothing can destroy it."

Upon being informed by the Almighty that the physical world I had so much believed in didn't really exist, I sat
back down on the barstool in fear that I was going to black
out. Tucker and Sidekick both saw what was going on and
came over to my side. God told Jesus to give me another
drink and then Tucker cracked a joke about the food he

ordered while he and I were in Life Review, saying, "What did you think of that pizza with no cheese, Buddy? That wasn't real, either. Was that bad, or what?"

We all laughed and then I asked God a question. "So tell me," I said to the Almighty, "do you throw a party like this for everyone who crosses over, or just a select few?" I swallowed half of my drink, preparing for the trip back to Earth.

"Depends," he said. "Everyone on Earth has a different idea as to what Heaven is going to be like when they get here, so I do the best I can to accommodate their beliefs, whatever that may entail. In your case, Buddy, you came back here with the idea that Heaven was really screwed up, so I created things around here to reflect that experience for you. Now, when someone else returns expecting to see a Heaven that resembles that of what they read in the Bible, I own another house that offers that experience. Actually, I own many houses like this in Heaven, Buddy."

"But how can you find enough time to entertain everyone who comes back?" I asked.

"I don't know, but it must have something to do with being God," he said laughing. "Finish your drink, Wilde. This party is over for the time being and a doctor is preparing to go out and tell your daughter the terrible news."

With that I got off the barstool, thanked Tucker and Sidekick for watching over my life and then embraced God. Then, suddenly, I was rocketed out of Heaven, back to Earth.

*"Eternity is not something that begins
after we are dead. It is going on all the time.
We are in it now."*

Charlotte Perkins Gilman, *The Forerunner*

Last Supper

It's what's for dinner.

Fill a tall glass with ice. Add 1 oz. of vodka, 2 oz. of Chianti wine and 4 oz. of 7-Up. Garnish with an orange slice.

Resurrection

It'll bring you back.

Fill an old-fashioned glass with ice. Add 1 shot of gin and a dash of bitters. Garnish with a wedge of lime.

CHAPTER 11

We Have a Rhythm!

Leaving Heaven and then slamming back into my physical body was quite the experience. It felt like I jumped six inches off the bed when I came crashing in. I heard a woman freak out!

"O my God! Did you see that?"

A man spoke, "Get out of the way. Let me see the monitor…surprise, surprise…we have a rhythm! Yeah…I love it when that happens!"

The woman spoke, "I thought he was worm food."

"I know…he's lucky. Anytime you can come back into your body after the doctor has called the time of death, that's a good thing."

The woman spoke. "He's been gone for some time now. I can't wait to hear his story."

"Yep, we probably have another NDE'er on our hands, but I have no time for that nonsense. You stay with him. I'm going out to tell the others."

The woman started calling my name out loud.

"Buddy, Buddy, can you hear me?"

"I'm not deaf. Stop yelling!"

"Do you know where you are, Buddy?"

"In the hospital."

"Very good! Do you know what happened?"

"You wouldn't believe me if I told you."

"Try me."

"Okay. I think I died and went to Heaven."

"Oh, really. And what was that like?"

"Don't patronize me. I know how you doctors are. If something can't be proven, it doesn't exist."

"No, I'm a nurse, and it happened to me once." I silently thanked God for having me be greeted back on Earth by an enlightened woman.

"Compare notes then—did you see 'the light'?"

"It's awesome, Buddy."

"Did you meet God?"

"Did I ever. He's such a nut, totally insane!"

"What color pants did he have on, nurse?"

"Well, he wore a white robe, trimmed in gold."

"What's his favorite martini, then?"

"I think he called it a Nazarene."

"Cool! You've been there. Jesus says 'Hi.'"

"I thirst!"

John 19:28
As said by Jesus Christ on the Cross

"Woe to you who get up early in the morning to go on long drinking bouts that last till late at night, woe to you drunken bums."

Isaiah 5:11
The Living Bible

Shouting Evangelist

"As seen on TV."

In an old-fashioned glass with ice, add 2 shots of Bailey's Irish Cream, 1 shot of Myers's Dark Rum, 1 shot of Bacardi Light Rum, 1 shot of Frangelico hazelnut liqueur. Top with a splash of 7-Up.

Bible Thumper

Quote a verse from the Bible with every sip.

In an old-fashioned glass, add 1½ tablespoons of sugar and 3 wedges of lime. With the blunt end of a butter knife, mash, pound, or thump limes until liquefied. Fill with ice and then add 2 shots of citrus vodka. Mix well by pouring the drink back and forth into equal sized glasses to dissolve sugar. Fresh lemon or orange may be used in place of lime.

Guilty Catholic

"I confess."

In a glass of ice, mix 1½ shots of Southern Comfort with 4 oz. of cranberry juice. Add a splash of lime seltzer and garnish with a wedge of lime.

"All the world's a stage, and all the men and women merely players."

William Shakespeare, *As You Like It*, Act II, Scene 7